IN GRATITUDE FOR

JOHN

WHO DIED, " A FINE NAVIGATOR," IN NORTH AFRICA,

ON THE 30TH AUGUST, 1943

AGED 20

KNOWING HOW TO LIVE

CONTENTS

		Page
I. RAHAB OF JERICHO [1405 B.C.]		7
II. HELEN OF ALEXANDRIA [260 B.C.] . . .		33
Note		54
III. OHAD'S WOMAN [A.D. 27]		55
IV. CHOSEN PEOPLE [A.D. 48]		73
Note		96
V. FIRST CORINTHIANS [A.D. 57]		97
Note		116
VI. HOLYEST ERTH [A.D. 61]		117
Note and Apology		138
VII. ALL THINGS ARE POSSIBLE [A.D. 68] . . .		139
VIII. FAREWELL, JERUSALEM [A.D. 69] . . .		159
Note		180

ACKNOWLEDGMENTS

To many of my friends (including my sons), I am under obligation for helpful suggestions made after kindly reading one or more of these plays in typescript. I am additionally indebted to Donald Finlayson, who gave *Ohad's Woman* a beautiful first production, and who, as I write, is rehearsing his Finlayson Players for a first performance of *Holyest Erth*. There must be a great number of books from which I have been " brain-picking " over a longish period, for purposes now apparent. I regret that I cannot thank the authors individually. Instead, with some diffidence, I will here thank one to whom I am personally a stranger for the message of his book, *Communion in the Messiah*, which reached me only after all these plays had been written. Perhaps here and there, in the following pages, echoes may be found of a hope to which the author of that book, Lev Gillet, an Orthodox Russian Christian, has given most noble expression.

H. F. R.

February, 1944.

HATED SERVANTS

HATED SERVANTS

Eight One Act Plays

by

H. F. RUBINSTEIN

" If the world hateth you, ye know that it hath hated me before it hated you. If ye were of the world, the world would love its own. . . . Remember the word that I said unto you, A servant is not greater than his master. If they persecuted me, they will also persecute you."—St. John xv. 18–20.

" The Lord setteth free the soul of his servants; and none of them that trust in him shall be desolate."—Psalm xxxiv.

LONDON

VICTOR GOLLANCZ LTD

1944

Acting editions of *All Things are Possible* and *First Corinthians* are available, the former published by Samuel French, Ltd. (26 Southampton Street, Strand, London, W.C.2), the latter by H. F. W. Deane & Sons (31 Museum Street, London, W.C.1), to whom applications regarding these two plays should respectively be addressed. Applications in respect of any of the remaining plays should be addressed to the League of British Dramatists, 84 Drayton Gardens, London, S.W.10.

Printed in Great Britain by the Camelot Press Limited
London and Southampton

RAHAB OF JERICHO

CHARACTERS

DOGUL, Ruler of Jericho

CALEB
PHINEHAS } Hebrew Spies

RAHAB

BASHEMATH, Rahab's Mother

Two Canaanite Soldiers

Scene: Interior of Rahab's house on the wall of Jericho
Time: An afternoon in the autumn of the year 1405 B.C.

THE ARGUMENT

And Joshua sent out two men as spies secretly, saying, Go view the land, and Jericho. And they went, and came into the house of an harlot whose name was Rahab, and lay there. And it was told the King of Jericho, saying, Behold there came men in hither to-night of the children of Israel to search out the land. And the King of Jericho sent unto Rahab, saying, Bring forth the men that are come to thee, for they be come to search out all the land. And the woman took the two men and hid them; and she said, Yea, the men came unto me, but I wist not whence they were; and it came to pass about the time of the shutting of the gate, when it was dark, that the men went out; whither the men went I wot not: pursue after them quickly; for ye shall overtake them. But she had brought them up to the roof, and hid them with the stalks of flax, which she had laid in order upon the roof. And as soon as they which pursued after them were gone out, she came up unto them upon the roof, and she said unto the men, I know that the Lord hath given you the land, and that your terror is fallen upon us and that all the inhabitants of the land melt away before you; for your God is God in heaven above and on earth beneath. Now therefore, since I have dealt kindly with you, deal kindly with my father's house, and save alive my father and my mother, and my brethren, and my sisters, and all that they have. And the men said unto her, Our life for yours if ye utter not this our business. Then she let them down by a cord through the window: for her house was upon the town wall, and she dwelt upon the wall. And she said unto them, Get you to the mountain, lest the pursuers light upon you; and hide yourselves there three days, until the pursuers be returned: and afterward may ye go your way. And the men said unto her, Behold, when we come into the land, thou shalt bind this line of scarlet thread in the window which thou didst let us down by: and thou shalt gather unto thee in the house thy father, and thy mother, and thy brethren, and all thy father's household. And it shall be that whosoever shall be with thee in the house, his blood shall be on our head, if any hand be upon him. And she said, According unto your words, so be it. And they departed. (From the Book of Joshua, Chapter II.)

By faith the harlot Rahab perished not with them that believed not. (From the Epistle to the Hebrews, Chapter XL.)

Reception room in RAHAB's *hostelry on the wall of Jericho. Bright scarlet curtains, draping the walls, set the tone of the establishment. A window or hole in the centre of the rear wall looks out on to a mountainous landscape. There are four exits: (1) back right, the outer door of the house, (2) front right, opening into the kitchen, (3) front left, giving access to* RAHAB's *apartment, and (4) back left, a passage leading to the other rooms, and via a ladder on to the roof of the house. Against the wall between exits (3) and (4) is an altar bearing a clay figurine of the goddess Astarte, the Teraphim of the house. Before the window is a portable side-table on which is laid a tray holding a large wine jar and some cups. A divan matching the curtains occupies the centre of the stage, a low stool before it. A mat or two for extra seating if it will help the producer.*

[CALEB, *a middle-aged, austere-looking countryman, stands by the window, gazing into the distance. He turns at a sound outside exit 1, whence presently emerges* BASHEMATH, *a stout, elderly woman, sombrely attired, carrying an enormous bundle of long stalks loosely strung together and panting violently from her exertions.*

BASHEMATH: Drat these steps ! What a climb ! (*Seeing* CALEB.) Excuse me, sir. I didn't notice you. (*Addressing the Teraphim.*) Mother Ashtoreth, give me my breath ! (*She deposits herself and bundle on the divan.*) That's better ! Rahab's engaged with a customer, I suppose ?

CALEB: I believe so.

BASHEMATH: Well, I can wait. I'm her mother. What's left of me ! And one thing I'd like to know is why, with half the houses in Jericho to choose from, my Ray had to go and plant herself right on the top of the city wall like this. Talk about living on the edge of a precipice ! But there, it's none of my business.

CALEB: You get a good view from here.

BASHEMATH: Good view ! What, that old mountain ? You're a stranger, perhaps ?

CALEB: Yes, I arrived only yesterday.

BASHEMATH: I thought I hadn't seen you here before. (*Confidentially.*) I like your face ! Look, I've tramped all the way from East Street with this load of flax. It's for my daughter's store. She doesn't forget her old mother, so I'm always glad to make her a little return when I can. And I'm going to lay it out in the sun for her. Have you ever been up there on the roof ? If it's a view you're after——

CALEB: You would like me to give you a hand?

BASHEMATH (*rising*): Anyone could see you were a real gentle-man! It's that rickety old ladder bothers me! If you wouldn't mind taking the bundle now. (*He proceeds to do so.*) You'll find it a bit damp, I dare say. The stalks have been soaking in water all night, but they'll dry all right once they're in the sun. I'll lead the way, shall I?

[*She does so, and he follows her out of exit 4, with the bundle already beginning to come to pieces. There is a short pause, then* RAHAB *appears from her room, followed by* DOGUL. *She is perhaps thirty, trim, wiry and inwardly alive behind a mask of cynicism: she wears her "glad rags" and gewgaws without ostentation.* DOGUL, *in the early forties, has personality, as well as physique, and would be a fine specimen of a man if he had any character.*

RAHAB: You'll have a drink before you go? (*She crosses to the table, and pours out.*)

DOGUL (*moving after her*): I haven't any money for you.

RAHAB: I didn't expect you would have. (*She hands him his cup, and pours out for herself.*)

DOGUL: I'll make it all up to you one of these days.

RAHAB: Naturally. When your official consorts have learnt how to run the household economically—isn't that it? What a hope! (*She lifts her glass, and they drink.*)

DOGUL: You are good to me, Rahab—but I think you might show me a little respect occasionally.

RAHAB: Do you? Well, your ruthlessness impresses me. And your conversation amuses me, sometimes.

DOGUL: Sometimes. Not to-day, for example. Well, you can hardly expect me to be at my best with my present load of responsibilities.

RAHAB: Gracious, what are you responsible for now?

DOGUL: The safety of Jericho. That's all.

RAHAB: I wouldn't let a trifle like that worry me.

DOGUL: How anyone can be so flippant in face of a crisis of this dimension——!

RAHAB: Is there another crisis? Do tell me all about it. (*She drinks.*) We're going to war again, I suppose?

DOGUL: Going to war? War's coming to us this time, my child —and not a pleasant war, believe me! These Hebrew vermin——

RAHAB: Oh, not the old Hebrews! Must I really listen to the entire history over again? How the Hebrew vermin escaped from

Egypt, and how they outwitted the mighty Pharaoh, and the way they crossed the Red Sea, and the slaughter they inflicted on the Amalekites and the Midianites and the Moabites, and what they did to Sihon of Heshbon and Og of Bashan——

DOGUL (*in a choking voice*): That's enough, I think.

RAHAB: Good. Then we're agreed for once. . . . Another cup? (*As she pours out for him.*) Hold it steady now! If you only knew how tired I am of your pet subject! I'll believe anything you like about these Hebrews, so long as you'll refrain from talking about them!

DOGUL (*after a drink*): Amazing! And it isn't as if you were lacking in intelligence. On the contrary, you've got quite a good brain for a woman.

RAHAB: Your compliments are always so touching. (*She drinks.*)

DOGUL: And you can go on calmly drinking and frivolling with the threat of imminent annihilation hanging over us——

RAHAB (*more seriously*): Annihilation. I like the sound of that!

DOGUL: Do you? Then it will no doubt come as good news to you that the murderous gang I am not allowed to mention are on the point of crossing the Jordan, and investing this city! Which I guarantee will hold out not longer than a week. I suppose you are quite unaware that the population is in a state of panic.

RAHAB: I had noticed signs, now you mention it. . . . Is there anything I can do about it? (*She stoops to pick up a stalk of flax.*) Mother's been here! Dear old thing, she has to deposit a trail of litter wherever she goes! (DOGUL *throws up his hands. At that moment*, BASHEMATH *re-appears from exit 4.*) Hullo, Mum. Sweet of you to bring me all that flax.

BASHEMATH: However did you find out——? (*Seeing* DOGUL.) I beg your pardon, my lord. (*Drawing back.*) I mustn't interrupt you, dearie.

RAHAB: It's all right. Dogul's just going. (*To* DOGUL.) Have you met my mother?

BASHEMATH (*obsequiously*): It's a very great honour for me, I'm sure. . . . (*But* DOGUL *has wandered away.*) Such lovely big stalks I've brought you, Ray. I picked them myself yesterday, and we gave them a good soaking overnight. And now I've laid them all out on the roof.

RAHAB: I wonder you found room.

BASHEMATH: I know you've got plenty without it, dearie, but what I say is you never know when a little extra flax mayn't come in useful. And I only wish I could afford to give you something better, as you're always so good to all of us. (*She is becoming tearful.*)

RAHAB (*firmly*) : Not now, Mum, please.

BASHEMATH : Sorry, dear. Oh, and I ought to mention I left a gentleman up there. He's a new friend of yours, I think. Such an interesting man.

DOGUL (*half listening*) : Would that be the ferocious looking oaf I passed on the steps as I was coming in ? (*He addressed the remark to* RAHAB.)

RAHAB : Well, I have two brand-new lodgers, so you can take your choice.

DOGUL : Brute with a great flaming red beard.

BASHEMATH : The gentleman I met hadn't got a beard.

RAHAB : Personally, I can't say I've noticed anything particularly interesting or ferocious about either of my lodgers.

DOGUL : The trouble with you is you never notice anything.

BASHEMATH : That's just what I say, my lord.

DOGUL (*ignoring her*) : Moreover, I don't at all approve of this latest whim of yours. No doubt it suits your pocket to supplement your professional earnings by taking in lodgers, as you call it, but, let me tell you, I regard it as a poor compliment that a house where I have been accustomed to resort for my entertainment should be transformed into a common hostelry.

RAHAB : How you exaggerate things, Dogul ! All this fuss about two dull and highly respectable foreigners—typical commercial travellers——

DOGUL : Choice company to offer me !

RAHAN : Have I offered you their company ? They're not company for anybody, as it happens : they're quiet as mice, don't even drink—perfect lodgers, in fact ! They actually offered to pay me cash down, without haggling !

DOGUL : Well, I call that suspicious.

BASHEMATH : So should I, my Lord. What I always say is——

DOGUL (*impatiently*) : Well, I can't waste any more of my time with you now. Just try and pull yourself together and think over what I've been telling you—before it's too late.

[*With a perfunctory nod, he departs from the house.*

BASHEMATH (*awed*) : Fancy meeting the Great Man here like that. At a time like this ! (RAHAB *remains silent.*) He's upset you, dearie. I can see that.

RAHAB (*shaking her head*): I know the animal too well for that!

BASHEMATH: "Animal"! That isn't a very respectful way to talk about our ruler.

RAHAB: King of Jericho! (*She laughs again.*)

BASHEMATH (*dropping on to the divan*): Life's just full of troubles, isn't it?

RAHAB: So it seems. Are you in a state of panic, Mother?

BASHEMATH: Panic?

RAHAB: About the Hebrew menace?

BASHEMATH: Oh, that. Well, if you want the truth, dearie, I've too many troubles nearer home. . . . But I mustn't take up any more of your precious time!

RAHAB (*resigned*): All right, Mum. I'm not expecting any visitors. (*She sits beside her.*) Tell me all about it.

BASHEMATH: I don't know where to begin, Ray. . . . And it isn't right of me, I know, to be always coming to you like this . . . but there, I've no one else to turn to, what with your father soaking himself in the tavern all day long, and you the only member of the family with a head screwed on tight. . . .

RAHAB (*patting her hand*): Have a drop of something to cheer you up, Mum.

BASHEMATH: Not for me, dearie. You keep it for your business friends.

RAHAB: Father can't last much longer. That'll be one worry the less.

BASHEMATH: Oh dear, and I know I shall miss him so! Funny, that, isn't it?

RAHAB: Sister Hatti's back on your hands again, I suppose?

BASHEMATH: Yes. You always did say no good would come of the marriage. He turned her out last night—bolted the door in her face, the dirty dog! Said he'd found out she was carrying on with his partner.

RAHAB: And was she?

BASHEMATH: I didn't ask any questions. You know how touchy she is. It's my belief he's known all along. If not, he was the only one in the street that didn't. I never did have much opinion of him. Fancy turning nasty like that in the middle of the night! Hatti's mad with him. And now Jaakan's upset because she wants his mattress back.

RAHAB: What, my old mattress.

BASHEMATH: That's right, dearie. Jaakan's been sharing it with Ari.

RAHAB: I gave it to Jaakan as a parting gift.

BASHEMATH: Well, he sold it to Hatti, or so she says. Only don't ask me to explain the rights and wrongs—they were going at it hammer and tongs when I came away. Poor Jaakan's not at all well, I'm sorry to say. He got his calling-up notice yesterday.

RAHAB: That's bad.

BASHEMATH: Jaakan of all people! Where's the sense of it, I say. What sort of soldier do they think they're going to make of him? He never did have any stomach for fighting.

RAHAB: Who wants to fight for Jericho, anyway!

BASHEMATH: Just what I say! Only what's the poor boy to do about it, Ray? I suppose you couldn't put in a word with one of your influential friends, duckie?

RAHAB: I might try.

BASHEMATH: It would take a weight off my mind, I can tell you that much. You've always been fond of Jaakan, now, haven't you?

RAHAB: Tell him I'll do what I can.

BASHEMATH: He can't expect you to do more than that, duckie.

RAHAB: It's rough luck on you, Mum—all this happening at once.

BASHEMATH: That's not all. I haven't told you the worst yet. (*She pauses.*)

RAHAB: Amar, I suppose.

BASHEMATH (*nodding*): I'm afraid she's going to have another baby, Ray.

RAHAB (*eloquently*): She would.

BASHEMATH: That'll be another mouth to feed.

RAHAB: And the rest of the business! Poor old Mum!

[*She puts her arm round her shoulder, and the old woman subsides into sobs.* RAHAB *lets her get it over.*

BASHEMATH (*drying her eyes*): I feel better now I've told you.

RAHAB (*rising*): You'll be wanting some money to go on with? (BASHEMATH *now feels decidedly better. Suddenly.*) Damn! I've just remembered. I lent my last shekel to—someone I probably shall never see again. (*Her mother's face falls.*) Don't worry. I'll raise the wind somehow.

BASHEMATH: You're too liberal with your money, dearie. That's always been your failing. (*A pause.*) You're not earning as much as you used to, are you, Ray?

RAHAB (*sharply*): Who says so?

BASHEMATH: Well, dearie, isn't it only to be expected? You haven't exactly gone out of your way to improve your position, have you, now? (*Warming to a favourite grievance.*) Giving up a lovely establishment right in the middle of the principal thoroughfare to come and bury yourself away in this bird's nest! Anyone might think you'd wanted to throw away all your old connection!

RAHAB: Must we have that all over again, Mother? (*Grimly.*) I can always earn more when I want to.

BASHEMATH: Don't you be so sure of it, my girl. We're none of us growing any younger, remember! And there's another thing. Nobody ever sees you at the sanctuary nowadays. You used to worship there regularly.

RAHAB: It used to mean something to me.

BASHEMATH: Be careful what you're saying, dearie. Remember, She (*pointing to the Teraphim*) may be listening.

RAHAB (*with a laugh*): That lump of clay! Do you really believe all that stuff and nonsense?

BASHEMATH (*shocked*): Hush, dear! What I say is, you can't know for sure and it doesn't cost you anything to be on the safe side. And it never did you any harm in the old days, did it, now? Of course, if you just don't care what happens——

RAHAB (*depressed*): I'm sorry to be such a disappointment to you, Mother.

BASHEMATH: All right, dearie. We'll all manage somehow, I dare say. And perhaps these new lodgers of yours will bring you luck.

RAHAB: My lodgers! Why ever didn't I think of them before?

BASHEMATH (*eagerly*): Haven't they paid you yet? (*As* RAHAB *shakes her head.*) There, now! And one of them in the house all the time we've been gossiping here! Do you think you could touch him for a bit—and let me have it, to go on with?

RAHAB: You shall have all I can get out of him, and welcome. I can always manage on credit—in spite of my fading charms.

BASHEMATH: You're too good to me, Ray; you really are. . . . Would you like me to go and call him now? Then I can be off home directly after.

RAHAB: Better stay and take pot-luck with me.

BASHEMATH: Do you really mean that, Ray? Wouldn't I just love to! And why shouldn't I give myself a treat for once, with both the girls at home? . . .

RAHAB (*listening*): There's someone coming down the ladder. . . .

BASHEMATH: That'll be him, all right. . . . I'll just pop into the kitchen, shall I? (*On her way there.*) Mind you make him stump up! Come and tell me as soon as he's gone, won't you, dear? (*As she disappears,* CALEB *enters quietly from the opposite side.*)

RAHAB (*returning his bow*): You are looking for something?

CALEB: For my friend. He has not returned?

RAHAB: I have not seen him. (*As he turns to withdraw.*) You need not go away.

CALEB: Did you want to speak to me?

RAHAB: Yes. Just a word. (*Plunging.*) You'll remember you offered to pay me yesterday, and I said it would do later.

CALEB: You would like me to pay you now? (*He takes out a purse.*)

RAHAB: If it is convenient. Two pieces, we agreed, I think.

CALEB: That is correct. (*He hands her two coins.*)

RAHAB (*recoiling*): But—these are gold shekels!

CALEB: You are in need of money, I think.

RAHAB: But, look here, I don't understand. . . . For just board and lodging? Unless—you are wanting something else?

CALEB: No, it was not for your body. It was for something in your eyes. It is an offering.

RAHAB: Well, I don't know what to say. Except thank you. It happens that my mother is in need of money. So I accept your present gratefully.

CALEB: It is as I thought. Gold to gold.

RAHAB: Are you laughing at me?

CALEB: Why should I laugh? When I can see you are near to crying.

RAHAB (*looking at him*): What a strange person you are.

CALEB: I feel myself a stranger in this city.

RAHAB: Where do you come from?

CALEB: You asked me yesterday. I told you: from Egypt.

RAHAB: You are not an Egyptian.

CALEB: Did I claim to be one? And you—what are you? A native of Jericho!

RAHAB: I'm a bit of a mixture, it seems. My mother is a Hittite, and my father an Amorite.

CALEB (*to himself*): A flower in the wilderness. A mystery.

RAHAB: But what about yourself? You haven't told me anything.

CALEB: My name is Caleb.

RAHAB: And the name of your people?

CALEB: We are a people of many names.

RAHAB: That isn't playing fair!

CALEB: Judah is one name. It is the name of my tribe. We are a brotherhood of tribes. (*Pause.*) Have you heard of Israel?

RAHAB: No.

CALEB: We call ourselves the Children of Israel.

RAHAB: Israel. I will remember the name. You are proud of it, are you not?

CALEB: I am proud to belong.

RAHAB (*miserable*): That must be wonderful: not to feel you are—dirt.

CALEB: Dirt? (*Slowly.*) I believe I have never met so good a woman as you before.

RAHAB: Good? What does that mean? I am fairly accomplished at my trade, if you call that good.

CALEB: I call it good to sacrifice yourself for others.

RAHAB: What extraordinary language you use! And how little you know about me! Sacrifice, indeed! I have always been fond of my mother, and there isn't much I wouldn't do for anyone I care about. That's only natural.

CALEB: You mean, you have been made like that?

RAHAB: Have I been made? Who made me? And what a waste of labour!

CALEB: So you can laugh at yourself? Yet you are in despair.

RAHAB (*passionately*): Because I cannot have my desires! You say I have been made: if so, it was for a life of pleasure, not of sacrifice! (*As he would protest.*) Wait! Of my trade I do not speak, because that is an abomination. But if I were free—really free to do as I please—a life of pleasure would be my choice! It would suit me. It's the truth, I tell you.

CALEB: Would it satisfy you?

RAHAB: What else is there for satisfaction? Tell me that, child of Israel.

CALEB: There is much else.

RAHAB: Not in Jericho.

CALEB: Does living in Jericho suit you? (*She shrugs her shoulders.*) You know no other way of living, perhaps? How should you?

RAHAB: Know? I know only what has happened to me. Once I thought I had found a wholly satisfying way of living. I thought I had escaped from Jericho! (*She controls a rising emotion before proceeding.*) I fell in love. I was young and foolish, and it was an interesting experience. It was as if I were a plant exposed to a strong sun and growing in it. Pleasure didn't mean anything to me while it lasted. It didn't last long. I found that what had sustained me in the light and heat of the sun was a mirage, a lie. I had been living in a dream. And waking up wasn't pleasant. It nearly finished me, but it taught me something. No more dreaming for me. Pleasure at least is *safe*.

CALEB: You are wrong. Loving is safe.

RAHAB: Not the kind I know.

CALEB: Loving with the whole mind and heart and strength.

RAHAB: So you yourself have loved?

CALEB: So my people love.

RAHAB: If it isn't a dream, you are lucky.

CALEB: Oh yes, we are lucky. (*A pause.*)

RAHAB: Where is this Israel? (*He hesitates.*) Where do you live?

CALEB (*slowly*): We live in I AM.

RAHAB: I never heard of the place.

CALEB: It isn't a place.

RAHAB: What, then?

CALEB: Ought I to tell you? And would you understand? How could anyone in Jericho understand?

RAHAB: Won't you try me?

CALEB: I AM is a name for that which cannot be named. I AM is God.

RAHAB (*disappointed*): Oh, your God. The Baal of Israel. (*Dully.*) That's very interesting.

CALEB: No, not *a* God. *God.* The one God. Our God and your God. The King over all. (*She is listening with close attention.*) King of every nation on earth, and of the Heavens outside the earth. A King who makes Himself known in the heart, though He cannot be seen with the eye. An invisible King. . . . Does all that sound nonsense? (*She shakes her head.*) Speak, then—truthfully.

RAHAB (*carried away*): Invisible—but—in the heart. . . . Let me hold fast to that ! (*She sways.*) It is all that I have glimpsed, and guessed at, in secret, since I was a child. (*She sinks on to the divan.*) And I thought *that* was a dream—or pretended to think it. . . . (*She closes her eyes.*) Tell me more about the King.

CALEB: He is a King in whom all truth and all goodness live for ever, whose ways are beyond our comprehending, whose servants fear Him even while they love Him with their whole being, and are loved by Him as a father loves his own children. He is a King with a purpose for us, a King that can fill every human life with His purpose.

RAHAB (*opening her eyes again*): A purpose, a real purpose ? Tell me the purpose ?

CALEB: As yet we are but children, and cannot see clearly. We know that for Israel there is a land provided, and a work to be done in that land. And we know that the work is holy.

RAHAB: Holy. *Holy.* Now I know what that means.

CALEB: It is a word of power. A word that can make, and can destroy, a word that can perform sheer impossibilities, in the strength of which (*he looks her straight in the eye*) a great sea will divide, and a multitude pass over on dry land.

[*She gives a gasp. They remain for some moments with eyes riveted.*

RAHAB (*steadily*): Holy. It is a good word. I like the cleanness of it. I feel in it all that in Jericho is not. (*In sudden exultation.*) At the sound of that word, I think the walls of Jericho will shake.

CALEB (*in a strange voice*): I think so too.

RAHAB (*drawing herself up*): If I were the King of the Heavens and earth, I would destroy Jericho utterly, utterly !

CALEB: Hush ! (*The door from the kitchen is opening.*)

RAHAB (*as in a daze*): What have I been saying ? (BASHEMATH *has appeared.*) Did you want me, Mother ?

BASHEMATH (*drawing back*): It'll do later, when you're disengaged, dear. . . .

RAHAB: I'm coming now. (*To* CALEB.) You have given me much to think about.

[CALEB *remains motionless as she follows her mother back to the kitchen. Still* CALEB *does not stir: until presently a sound from without the house brings him to himself with a jerk, leading to a new tension as he advances anxiously towards the front door.*

CALEB (*calling*): Phinehas ! . . . At last !

[There is a faint answering shout, and a moment later PHINEHAS *bursts in, out of breath. He is a younger man, coarser-grained, with a bushy red-beard, and a brisk, hearty manner.*

PHINEHAS: I've been running. . . . (*He holds on to him for support.*) Wait till I get my wind. . . . (*His panting subsides.*) Sorry to have kept you waiting all this time. My impatience got the better of me, after all !

CALEB: You continued the circuit alone ?

PHINEHAS: I've finished the whole job. I couldn't resist it. Here you are ! (*He pulls out of an inner pocket a plan drawn on a folded skin.*) I've filled in the measurements—all but the last few. I've got *them* here ! (*Tapping his forehead.*) And I've found three more large cracks—there, there and there. (*Indicating the points on the plan.*)

CALEB: Well done !

PHINEHAS: Don't be too sure ! (*As he puts the plan away.*) It would have been better done if I'd waited till the morning, as you advised. I may have made a hash of everything.

CALEB (*quickly*): What's happened ?

PHINEHAS: I had the line out, making the final measurements; the ramparts were deserted, and everything had gone smoothly up till then. Too smoothly, I suppose. I happened to turn my head, and there was a little weasel of a fellow creeping along the parapet not twenty paces away.

CALEB: Did he have a clear view of you ?

PHINEHAS: Clear enough. Fortunately, I kept my head.

CALEB: He followed you, of course?

PHINEHAS (*nodding*): And I led him a dance ! But he stuck to it gamely—I'll say that for him—right to the top of Spring Hill. Then I gave him the slip all right. (*He chuckles.*) He'll have a headache wondering where I got to from there !

CALEB (*thinking quickly*): They'll have a watch on the gate.

PHINEHAS: Probably. And kicking myself won't help, I know ! So there it is. We're safe enough here as long as we keep indoors, but we can't stay here for the rest of our lives, eh ? Besides, there'll be gossip, and that'll reach our landlady's ears.

CALEB: We needn't worry about her.

PHINEHAS: I don't agree with you. With people coming in and out——

CALEB: Never mind about that, I say. But the sooner we get away the better. We'll have to make a bolt for it. It's not going to be easy.

PHINEHAS: I suppose I might disguise myself?

CALEB (*tickled*): As a tender maiden, eh? . . . We'd better wait till it begins to get dark. Just before the gate closes. (*With a glance out of the window.*) We'll have time to mark up the plans before we get our things together. . . . (*As the other produces his plan.*) No, not in here. Take it into our room.

[*They are moving towards exit 4 when* RAHAB *re-appears from the kitchen.*

PHINEHAS: Hullo, mistress! We were just talking about you. We've got to be moving on.

RAHAB (*quickly, looking to* CALEB): When?

CALEB: Before nightfall.

RAHAB: So soon? But (*desperately*) I must talk to you!

CALEB: Presently. You were not going out?

RAHAB: No. (*She steadies herself.*) Mother is making some broth. You'll stay for that?

CALEB: If the sun allows. . . . Come, Phinehas. (*He leads him off back left.*)

RAHAB (*looking after him*): If the sun allows. . . . I must decide this for myself!

[*Her glance, shifting, falls on the Teraphim, and she recoils in sudden disgust. Then, turning aside, she falls on her knees.*

RAHAB (*murmuring urgently*): I AM. (*She closes her eyes.*) Father . . . Holy One . . . King of Heaven and earth . . . Help me to do Thy will. Help me to serve.

[*She rises to her feet, hastily, at the sound of men's voices approaching from exit 1. A moment later,* DOGUL *bursts in with a drawn sword, followed by two degenerate looking soldiers, armed with spears. He is in a state of fury, largely dictated by fear.*

DOGUL (*seeing Rahab*): Ha! There she is—unconcerned as ever! (*Aggressively.*) Where are those lodgers of yours?

RAHAB (*faintly*): My lodgers? (*Thinking hard.*) Whatever's the matter with you, Dogul?

DOGUL: None of that! Answer my question, woman, or I'll have you stoned! Don't stand there gaping at me. Where are the men, I say?

RAHAB: They've gone out I think, my lord.

DOGUL: Think, do you? You'd better think again—quickly. Do you know what they are—where they've come from?

RAHAB: From Egypt, they told me

DOGUL: From Egypt! They told you that, did they? From Egypt, and no mistake! Filthy Hebrews—Hebrew spies—that's what they are!

RAHAB: Dogul! That's serious, isn't it?

DOGUL: Serious! By Ashtoreth, wait till I catch them! Out, you say they are—both of them?

RAHAB: Now I remember—they may have returned. . . .

DOGUL (*advancing*): Well, while you're making up your mind about it——

RAHAB (*quickly*): Wait! You'd better let me go and fetch them for you. I can get their arms away first, then you'll have no trouble with them. They'll fight like lions, so long as they're armed. (*As this goes home.*) If I know my business, it oughtn't to take me long! (*With a gesture towards the wine.*) Won't you be warming yourself up, my lord?

[*This settles the question. He is already helping himself as she disappears by exit 4.*

FIRST SOLDIER (*sotto voce*): Did you hear what she said, Sergeant? They'll fight like lions, she said.

SECOND SOLDIER: Well, what do you expect of Hebrews? Think they'd fight fair, like decent Canaanites? Lot of dirty, slimy monsters, that's what they are. Everyone knows it. Ain't that correct, sir?

DOGUL (*after his first cup, soberly enough*): They know how to fight— and don't you forget it, either! (*As he pours himself out a second cup.*) Where are the rest of your men?

SECOND SOLDIER: You told me to post them outside the house, sir.

FIRST SOLDIER: Shall I go and call them up, sir? (*He edges towards exit 1.*)

DOGUL: Stay where you are, louse! I can call them myself if I want them, can't I? (*A moment later.*) Get over to that door, both of you (*pointing to exit 4*) and keep your ears open! (*Calling behind him.*) Hi there! Get ready to re-inforce us!

FIRST SOLDIER (*as they take up their stations*): We should be all right, if she's got their arms away.

DOGUL: I want them alive, if they don't resist, remember.

Second Soldier: Yes, sir. (Dogul *continues to drink. To his companion.*) Trust her to know how to manage the bastards. She could manage you and me easily enough, I reckon.

First Soldier (*excitedly*): I hear footsteps, sir.

Dogul: Where are your spears, you blockheads !

[*They hold them at the ready as the door opens, and* Rahab *returns alone.*

Rahab: They're not there, that's certain. I've looked on the roof as well. I'd better try the kitchen next.

Dogul (*muttering*): Wait till I catch them, that's all ! I'll teach the mongrels !

Rahab: You might be having a look in my room, Dogul—just to make sure they're not skulking there listening all the time.

[*She passes into the kitchen.* Dogul *pours out more wine with a trembling hand.*

Dogul (*calling*): Sergeant ! Take your man into that room (*pointing to exit 3*)—search it carefully. (*He takes a gulp.*) At once ! Do you hear me ? (*With eloquent looks, the men proceed gingerly in the direction indicated.*) Look particularly behind the door. (*As they disappear, he backs carefully towards exit 1, shouting*) Stand by, there below! (*He turns with a violent start as* Rahab *emerges from the kitchen.*)

Rahab: It's only me ! They're not in the kitchen. (*The two soldiers return from her room.*) Not in there either, eh ? Then we've looked everywhere. They must have left the house, after all.

Dogul: Why couldn't you have said so at first—instead of giving us all this trouble for nothing ?

Rahab: I apologize. (*She goes to the table, and takes the wine jar.*) Perhaps your men would like something to drink before you go ?

First Soldier (*jumping to it*): Thirsty work it's been, ma'am, and no mistake.

Dogul (*draining his cup*): Who said we were going ?

First Soldier: We're in no hurry, ma'am. (*As* Rahab, *disconcerted, fills his cup.*) Thankee, ma'am. (*Drinking.*) Your very good health !

Second Soldier (*taking his turn*): Don't you worry, ma'am. We'll look after you. They'll just drop into our hands if we wait here long enough.

Dogul (*having finished his drink*): Silence, you dogs ! Put those cups down ! (*The men swallow hastily before obeying.*) We will now complete our investigation. (*To* Rahab.) You say you've searched the roof of the house ?

RAHAB: Every inch of it.

DOGUL: Are you sure they weren't hiding anywhere?

RAHAB: Quite sure. I looked most carefully.

DOGUL (*dramatically*): Follow me, men of Jericho! To the roof!

[*Brandishing his sword and muttering imprecations, he leads them off unsteadily by exit 4 before* RAHAB *can stop him. With the coast clear,* BASHEMATH *steals in from the kitchen.*)

BASHEMATH: That's put the fat in the fire, hasn't it? (RAHAB *turns to her, mutely, for support.*) What have you done with them, love?

RAHAB: Smothered them in your flax, Mum. You said it would come in useful.

BASHEMATH: The light's none too good; that's something.

[*It has begun to darken.*

RAHAB: And Dogul's pretty well soused. The jar's nearly empty! (*She replaces it on the table.*)

BASHEMATH: Well, there's a chance. . . . Fancy them being Hebrews all the time! Well, if you're on their side, good luck to them, I say! But I'd like to know what you think you're going to do with them if they're not copped up there. You'll get yourself into a proper mess, one of these days, dearie. His lordship's cross enough as it is.

[*A crash off.*

RAHAB (*starting*): Whatever was that? (*She goes to look.*)

BASHEMATH: Someone missing his step on the ladder, if you ask me! (DOGUL'S *voice, swearing loudly, is heard off.*)

RAHAB: You're right. It's Dogul—coming back. (*She draws away from the door.*)

BASHEMATH: Empty-handed, eh?

RAHAB: And now I'm going to have some fun with him! Mind you back me up!

[DOGUL *re-appears from exit 4, rubbing his pate.*

DOGUL: That accursed ladder of yours! Might have broken my neck!

[*The two soldiers follow, hiccupping in their efforts to preserve straight faces.*

RAHAB (*coolly*): Well, I said you wouldn't find them up there, didn't I? And now, if you'll only listen patiently, I can tell you perhaps where you *will* find them.

DOGUL: What the——? Do you mean to say you knew all the time?

RAHAB: If I only had known! When I think of the dirty trick they've played me! To sneak away like that, without paying, after winning my confidence and borrowing all my savings! Mother saw them go. (*Addressing* BASHEMATH.) You're sure they had their pack with them?

BASHEMATH (*stoutly*): True as I'm standing here—every word of it!

RAHAB: It'll be a lesson, anyway. No more lodgers for me!

DOGUL (*to* BASHEMATH): And where have *you* sprung from, may I ask?

RAHAB: She was in the kitchen dozing in front of the fire. She must have dropped off just before I looked in there, because she remembers hearing you arrive, and she says it seemed to be soon after she saw the men making off. So you must have just missed them.

BASHEMATH (*intelligently*): That's right, dearie. They can't have gone far.

RAHAB: They've probably been waiting to slip out of the gate just before it closes.

BASHEMATH: When it's getting dark, you mean? Wouldn't that be artful of them, now! And suppose they got away from Jericho, where would they be making for, I'd like to know?

RAHAB: Well, if they're spies, they'd be wanting to get back to their camp, wouldn't they?

BASHEMATH: That's just over the Jordan, they say.

RAHAB (*to* DOGUL): If you get after them quickly, you could overtake them before they reach the fords.

DOGUL (*snappily*): When I want your advice I'll ask for it. (*To the* SECOND SOLDIER.) How many men have you got posted outside?

SECOND SOLDIER: Outside this house, sir? Eight or so.

DOGUL: Leave four of them and take the rest of the squad along with you. At the double, do you understand? I'll give you your orders as we go.

[*He drives them before him out of exit 1 without leave-taking.*

BASHEMATH: My broth!

[*She hurries into the kitchen, while* RAHAB *stands listening.*

RAHAB (*as* BASHEMATH *returns*): They're well away!

BASHEMATH: The broth is doing nicely too. . . . But we're not out of the wood yet, dearie, with soldiers stationed outside the house, remember.

RAHAB: At least they'll keep any customers away! I'll bolt the door, all the same, in case of accidents.

BASHEMATH (*while she is doing so*): Better leave your friends where they are for the night.

RAHAB: Too risky. The news will be all over the town by morning. I'm going to call them at once. (*As she crosses swiftly from exit 1 to exit 4.*) Bring the lamp out here, will you, Mother?

[*It has grown much darker. She goes out by exit 4.*

BASHEMATH: I'll bring the broth in as well, shall I? (RAHAB *has already disappeared. As she bustles into the kitchen.*) We mustn't let them leave hungry, after paying gold pieces!

[*She bustles back again before long with a lighted lamp, which she sets on the altar before the Teraphim. It is not a bright light, and the remainder of the play is characterized by shadowy figures moving in an atmosphere of semi-obscurity.* BASHEMATH *next fetches from the kitchen a steaming bowl of broth, which she deposits on the stool before the divan. Finally, she sets around it four smaller bowls, which will presently be dipped into the large one to be drunk from. Meanwhile, voices have been heard approaching from exit 4, and now* RAHAB *returns with the two Hebrews, carrying their pack, in her wake.*

PHINEHAS (*pleasurably excited*): Well, you've done us a good turn, mistress, and we aren't likely to forget it in a hurry.

BASHEMATH (*liking the look of him*) My, if it isn't the oaf with the red beard! And a beauty, too!

RAHAB: Don't be alarmed. It's only Mother. (*He bows respectfully.*) Your name is Phinehas, I think?

PHINEHAS: Ginger to my friends.

BASHEMATH: Then you'll fancy something to warm your inside, I dare say. (*She fills a small bowl.*)

PHINEHAS (*smacking his lips*): Hot broth! (*She hands him the bowl.*) Smells good, too! We are putting you ladies to a lot of trouble, I'm afraid.

BASHEMATH: Don't mention it. A pleasure, I'm sure. (*She fills another bowl.*) Where's your chum, now? (CALEB *is over by the window.*) Ah, there he is (*approaching him*), admiring the view, as usual! (*Handing him the bowl.*) Drink this up while it's hot, now. It'll do you good.

28

CALEB (*taking it*): Thanks. Not for the broth only. (*He peers out of the window.*) And it isn't the view I'm thinking about.

RAHAB (*joining them*): I know what he's thinking about. . . . Here's some for you, Mother. (*She has filled the other two bowls and gives one to* BASHEMATH. *Then, softly to* CALEB.) Patience. All is well.

CALEB: You know that?

RAHAB: By I AM's breath.

[*During the following speeches, all are engaged in sipping the hot broth.*

CALEB (*pointing through the window*): That breath—blows us out yonder.

RAHAB: It's a long drop, isn't it? And there's a steep slope at the bottom, remember.

CALEB: It's the only way out. That simplifies the question.

[PHINEHAS *has joined the conference.*

RAHAB: Yes. You'll have room to move out there. I'd keep well away from the fords for a day or two—three, to be on the safe side. You'll find plenty of cover on the mountain-side. The moon should be up presently, and there's a good track along to the right there.

CALEB: I've observed it. . . . Three days on the mountain. What do you say to the idea, Phin?

PHINEHAS: Sounds all right to me. Once we're on the other side of the wall. But how are we going to get there?

RAHAB: You can take my bedding—cut it into strips——

BASHEMATH (*shocked*): What, all your beautiful bedding, dearie?

RAHAB (*to the men*): I suppose you haven't a rope or cord of any kind?

PHINEHAS: Only our measuring line. It's in my pack.

CALEB: Get it out.

BASHEMATH (*standing by*): Give me your bowl, Ginger, and I'll get you some more broth.

PHINEHAS (*as she takes it from him*): Thank you, Ma. (*He rummages in the pack while she goes to re-fill the bowl.*)

RAHAB: Would the line be long enough?

PHINEHAS: Just right! I've measured, so I ought to know. (*He produces a coil of scarlet cord.*) Here we are!

RAHAB (*taking it from him*): Let me feel it. . . . I like the colour: matches my curtains ! (*Examining the cord.*) It's not very thick, is it ?

CALEB: We're neither of us heavyweights.

BASHEMATH (*who has returned with the steaming bowl*): Here, take this, Ginger ! (*As he does so.*) Now let me have a look at it. (*She takes and tests the cord expertly.*) Good flax ! That'll hold. I guarantee it. (*She hands it back to* CALEB.)

RAHAB: What my mother doesn't know about flax . . . !

BASHEMATH (*to* CALEB): Some more broth, sir ?

CALEB (*declining*): Thank you, but the sooner we're off the premises the better for everyone, I think.

RAHAB: You'll want to take some provisions with you. Go and see what's left in the larder, will you, Mum ?

BASHEMATH: I'll fill their water-bottles at the same time, shall I ?

PHINEHAS (*as he and* CALEB *unstrap their bottles*): Thinks of everything ! Isn't she a marvel ! (*She digs him in the ribs, and, after collecting the two water-bottles, departs to the kitchen.*) Now let's get to work. Where's that line ?

CALEB: Here.

PHINEHAS: Give me the end. (*He bends down, and proceeds to secure it to a leg of the table.*) One thing : whatever blunders we may have committed—some of us !—if ever we get safely back to camp again, nobody's going to say we haven't made a thorough job of this ! (*He rises.*) Here goes ! (*He releases the coil out of the window.*) And if we're lucky we'll get a nod and a grunt out of old Josh ! Isn't that right ?

CALEB: It wouldn't surprise me if he gave the order to advance the next day.

PHINEHAS: Just what I'm thinking. (*Peering down.*) That'll be just about touching bottom. (*Straightening himself.*) Three days in the open—one more to see us home—and the day after that——

RAHAB (*quietly*): And the day after that—you'll be coming back to massacre us all. And a good thing too, no doubt.

PHINEHAS (*turning to face her*): Now, look here, mistress ! The time's come for a little plain-speaking between us three. There's not going to be any misunderstanding about this. You've taken good care of us, and we intend to take good care of you when the day arrives. And that's a bargain ! What do you say, Caleb ?

CALEB: I say, my life for hers. Nothing less.

PHINEHAS: Mind you (*turning to* RAHAB), that's always providing no little secrets leak out after we've made our getaway. That's understood as well, I hope.

CALEB: There is understanding on all points between us. My life for hers, as God is my witness.

RAHAB: I'm not so sure that I want my life.

[BASHEMATH *returns from the kitchen with the water-bottles, and some provisions wrapped in a cloth.*

BASHEMATH: Well, I've done the best I could for you. Here are the water-bottles. (*The men catch them from her.*) Who's going to take charge of the fodder? (PHINEHAS *relieves her of the packet.*) You'll find some decent meat there, with a few loaves of bread and some figs.

RAHAB: I certainly don't want to live, if Mother's going to be killed?

BASHEMATH: What's all this? Who says I'm going to be killed?

RAHAB: Everyone in Jericho is going to be killed, Mother. (*Tensely.*) It has to be. (*A silence falls.*)

BASHEMATH (*slowly*): It's like that, is it? I've seen it coming.

PHINEHAS: You bring your mother along in here with you, and she'll be looked after the same as you. Don't you worry, old lady. Ginger isn't going to let you down!

BASHEMATH (*unsmiling*): And what about Dad—and her sisters and brothers and the little ones? Think I'd leave any of the family behind to save my own skin? No, thank you. It's all or none with me.

CALEB: Listen, Rahab. Your house is going to be singled out from every other house in Jericho. As soon as you hear our main body's over the Jordan—and you'll hear that in good time, I promise you—hang this line out of the window, just as it is now, and get your mother, and her whole family, to move into the house, with all their belongings. Once they're under this roof, we'll be answerable for them.

BASHEMATH: It'll be rather a squash, won't it!

RAHAB: And after that—what's to become of us?

CALEB: You'll be made welcome in our camp.

RAHAB: Even though we are not Hebrews?

CALEB (*looking at her*): You belong to Israel, I think.

RAHAB: Whatever that means, it sounds good to me.

BASHEMATH: It'll be a change, anyway—give us a fresh start, as you might say.

PHINEHAS: And till then—you won't utter a syllable—(*winking*) eh, Ma?

BASHEMATH: I know how to keep my mouth shut. (*Indicating* RAHAB.) She can tell you that.

PHINEHAS: Good enough. Then, if that's all settled—— (*He goes to the window.*)

BASHEMATH: Just itching to get away from us, isn't he! (*Examining the line.*) You're sure you've got that firmly fixed, now?

PHINEHAS: I'll pay for it if it isn't! (*Embracing her.*) There's a kiss for luck! Ready, Caleb? (*At a nod from the latter, he swings a leg over the ledge, grasping the line.*) So long, everybody! (*Commences to lower himself.*)

BASHEMATH: Carefully, now! Isn't he a lad!

CALEB (*at the window*): Give us a whistle when you've landed.

[PHINEHAS *waves his hand in answer, and disappears over the ledge. They all stand around rather breathless, till they hear a merry whistle from below.*

That's Phinehas! (*Advancing to* RAHAB.) We'll be meeting again before long.

RAHAB: You'll whistle too, won't you, when you've landed?

BASHEMATH: What about your pack? Don't say you'd forgotten it!

CALEB: I had—completely! Throw it after me, will you? We'll stand clear before I whistle. (*He takes* RAHAB's *hands.*) Well, you've saved our lives, landlady.

RAHAB: You've given me mine, I think.

[*He presses, then releases her hands, and, with a nod to* BASHEMATH, *mounts the window ledge.*

CALEB: God have mercy on us all.

[*He lowers himself out of sight without further words. The women peer out after him.*

BASHEMATH: The moon's rising! (*Presently there is a sustained whistle on a single note.* RAHAB *fetches the pack, and drops it out of the window.*) Look, there they are—waving to us!

[*Both women wave back, then* RAHAB *turns away with a new light in her eyes, as the curtain falls.*

HELEN OF ALEXANDRIA

CHARACTERS

JOSEPH, known as Theophilus
DEBORAH, his mother
SIMEON, his uncle
HELEN
LYSIAS, her brother

Scene: A house in the Jewish quarter of Alexandria
Time: Late spring of (about) 260 B.C.

The house belonged to DEBORAH's *late husband,* JOSEPH's *father, a well-to-do Jew of hellenized tastes. The study is furnished in Grecian style, adapted to harmonize with highly coloured Oriental decorations. The entrance is on the spectators' right. Against the opposite wall, a side-board and small side-table, chests serving as book-cases in the background.* SIMEON, *an elderly man, clean-shaven, but wearing the traditional black gown and skull-cap of a Rabbi, is seated at a table in the centre of the room, poring over an opened scroll, while he fondles a cat that has nestled on his shoulder. A couch and two or three chairs are arranged in the foreground.*

SIMEON (*to the cat*): Well, and what are we to make of that, Tobias?

[*The door opens and his sister* DEBORAH *enters, ushering in* HELEN, *an elegant and attractive girl in the early twenties, and her brother,* LYSIAS, *of no less gracious bearing and pleasant personality, some few years her senior.*

DEBORAH: May we come in?

SIMEON (*looking up*): Why, of course, sister. (*He rises, observing the visitors.*) Please—all of you.

DEBORAH (*advancing*): It's Helen and Lysias.

SIMEON: As I see. (*As they approach.*) Come to welcome our Theo, no doubt?

LYSIAS: With a thousand apologies for disturbing you all at this hour!

DEBORAH: What nonsense! Theo will be so delighted! Sit down, both of you—please! You'll have some refreshment?

HELEN: Nor for me, I beg!

LYSIAS: Not before I set eyes on old Theo!

35

HELEN (*seating herself*): He arrived at dawn, you say?

DEBORAH: Actually it was just before dawn. We were all in bed, of course—I never heard the knocking, even. Fortunately, Simeon is a light sleeper. You can imagine our joy! We weren't expecting him back till after our Pentecost Festival.

LYSIAS: So we had understood. Helen and I could hardly believe the news.

HELEN: We heard it only by the merest chance.

LYSIAS: Our kitchen-maid heard it from the milkman, to be exact! He never misses anything, that fellow!

HELEN: Dear Gorgo, in the middle of doing my hair, announced quite casually that she'd heard cook say that the Trade Delegation had returned from Syria.

LYSIAS: We *had* to come round just as we are. We were only afraid we might find Theo asleep after his journey.

DEBORAH: So he would have been, if I'd had my way! The poor boy had hardly undressed, before a summons arrived from the Palace. The whole Delegation was to breakfast with Pharaoh—in two hours! I say, Pharaoh or no Pharaoh, it was most inconsiderate!

HELEN: How was Theo looking? Tired out, I expect?

DEBORAH: Not too well, I must say. They had such awful weather, it seems, the whole way from Joppa. They embarked there I don't know how many days ago. Theo was sea-sick most of the time.

HELEN: So they broke the return journey, and visited Judea, as he had hoped?

DEBORAH: Yes, they were at Jerusalem for quite a number of days. . . . But—you'll excuse me, I know—I must just finish giving my orders downstairs. And please don't get up, either of you! (*She sees the cat.*) So there you are, Tobias! Did he want to come with me, then? (*She takes him in her arms.*) And was he glad to see our Theo safely home again? (*To* SIMEON, *who has opened the door for her.*) Thank you, Simeon. . . . I'll be back again presently.

[*She leaves.* SIMEON *resumes his seat. A pause.*

SIMEON (*to* HELEN): Will you not have this cushion, please? (*Passing it to her.*)

HELEN: Thank you, sir. But do continue your studies. We won't talk.

SIMEON: I would prefer that we talked together. About my studies, if you will.

36

LYSIAS: We should soon be out of our depth, I'm afraid, Rabbi.

SIMEON: I think not, my friend. . . . Perhaps I may be allowed to read you some words upon which I was pondering as you came in? (*As they assent, he reads.*) " The divine nature cannot communicate directly with man, but intercourse is carried on between God and man, both in our waking hours and in sleep, through the medium of love. . . ." (*He pauses.*) A profound thought.

LYSIAS: It sounds familiar. . . . Surely you cannot be quoting from the *Symposium*?

SIMEON: Correct! You seem surprised.

LYSIAS: Well, I am! To find a Jewish Rabbi reading Plato.

SIMEON (*smiling*): There is no law against it.

LYSIAS: I didn't think they would have heard of Plato in Jerusalem.

SIMEON: But this is not Jerusalem. This is Alexandria.

HELEN: You've lived here most of your life, haven't you?

SIMEON: Since I was a youngster of twelve. My sister and I were transported here after the Battle of Gaza.

HELEN: And Theo's father—did he arrive with you?

SIMEON: He was born here. His family were among the first settlers after your Alexander founded the city. His father could actually remember seeing the lighthouse built.

HELEN: I can't imagine Alex without a lighthouse. Can you, Lysias?

LYSIAS: And that was even earlier than the Museum, wasn't it? I certainly can't imagine Alex without her library.

SIMEON: We are fortunate to be living in such a fine city.

HELEN: Jerusalem is also a fine city, is it not?

SIMEON: In ancient times, it was so. We ask in our morning and evening prayers that its glories may one day be restored.

HELEN (*after a pause*): I would like so much to know—if you would tell us—about your holy city.

SIMEON: It was founded, like this city, by a soldier. He was a poet also. It was our King David. He chose to build his city on a high mountain called Zion, and his son, King Solomon, crowned it with the great Temple.

HELEN: You had kings in those days—Jewish kings?

SIMEON: Yes, my lady. At first good kings—afterwards too many bad kings.

HELEN: How ignorant I am ! Is your nation ages old, like this Egypt ?

SIMEON: Before we became a nation, we were a rabble of slaves in an Egypt ancient and mighty.

HELEN: What happened ?

LYSIAS (as SIMEON pauses): But, Helen—the Rabbi invited us to discuss Plato !

SIMEON (answering HELEN): Moses happened. To be exact, Moses, appointed by God, delivered our fathers from their bondage in Egypt, gave us the Torah, made of us a nation, sanctified us with the divine blessing and promise, whereby, at the time appointed, we entered and conquered our land . . . the land called Judea. That happened more than a thousand years ago.

HELEN: Under your king ?

SIMEON: The kings came later. They were not so important. Moses was a Prophet, the first and greatest of them. The Prophets were important.

LYSIAS: And the Torah—that you would say, would you not, is the most important thing of all ?

SIMEON (turning to him): You have some knowledge of our Scriptures ?

LYSIAS: Only from what Theo has told me. Once he tried to teach me your language—but it was too difficult.

SIMEON (with a sigh): Always that is the stumbling-block. If only there could be the same language everywhere ! God's word should be a gift to all alike. Why, there are actually Jewish children in this city of Alexandria who, because they have been taught to speak Greek, are growing up wholly ignorant of their Torah !

HELEN: What is the meaning of Torah, Rabbi ?

SIMEON: It is the holy teaching—whereby man may be made perfect.*

[HELEN (awed): Are all men good in Judea ?

SIMEON (with a heavy sigh): Alas ! how far from it ! A long schooling we must undergo and many hard lessons are to be learnt. Learnt and re-learnt, if need be: if a first punishment is not severe enough !

* The Rabbi is rather a bore, I fear. To account for Helen's later conduct, it seemed necessary to acquaint a modern audience with the history lesson she is absorbing. The following passage (square-bracketed) may be cut by any producer who thinks his public can do without it.

LYSIAS: You speak as if learning and punishment were the same thing, sir.

SIMEON: You have a careful ear !

HELEN (*after a pause*): Please explain.

SIMEON: Was it, for instance, a lesson or a punishment when our city was taken by Nebuchadnezzar, our Temple razed to the ground, and the last of our kings, with the flower of our nation, transported as prisoners to far away Babylon ? A punishment, certainly, for all manner of sinfulness. Yet by means of that punishment we learnt to know God better, I think.] (*He turns to Lysias.*) All this, I fear, can hold small interest for a Philosopher of the Garden.

LYSIAS: Frankly, sir, it is incomprehensible to me.

SIMEON: You mean, that God is incomprehensible ?

LYSIAS (*shaking his head*): What I fail to understand is how anyone living under the benign rule of King Ptolemy Philadelphus can be so strongly moved over such completely theoretical questions. I mean no offence, sir.

SIMEON: We Jews are made like that.

LYSIAS: Not all of you, surely ?

SIMEON: The Jew in all of us is the same.

LYSIAS: Not in Theo, with respect. Theo's mind is too well-balanced.

SIMEON: And so you think that Theo could set foot in the land of his fathers without feeling in his marrow the mysterious Power that has set that land apart—now exalted, now brought low.

LYSIAS: I should be surprised to learn that any such fancies even crossed his mind.

SIMEON (*deferentially*): You, as his greatest friend, should know best.

LYSIAS: What do you think, Helen ?

HELEN: Theo has always felt a deep concern for the welfare of fellow Jews.

LYSIAS: That's only natural. That isn't what the Rabbi meant.

SIMEON: No, that is quite different.

HELEN: Certainly he showed great eagerness when he spoke of the possibility of visiting Judea—but then he was so elated at the whole prospect.

LYSIAS: As well he might be ! To be appointed to the secretariat of one of Pharaoh's special delegations ! The lucky dog !

HELEN: There was no luck about it, Lysias. It was his brilliant work for the Ministry.

LYSIAS: I'm not denying it, my dear. I only wish I had a fraction of his skill as a negotiator. Theo's a man in a million.

SIMEON: There at least we are all in agreement!

HELEN (to SIMEON): And has the mission been successful?

SIMEON: That's what we are all wanting to know! We haven't had a chance to talk to him yet. In any case, before reporting to the Palace, his lips would be sealed.

LYSIAS: H'm! And in due course we shall be officially informed, no doubt, that " matters of common interest were frankly discussed, and a complete understanding was reached on all points "—which, being interpreted, means Business as Usual—until the next war breaks out!

HELEN: I hear voices! (*As does the audience.*) It's Theophilus!

[DEBORAH *returns, followed by* JOSEPH, *a youngish man, well-built, studious-looking, not conspicuously Jewish.*

DEBORAH: Here he is at last!

JOSEPH: Helen! (*He takes both her hands in his.*) Lysias! (*He embraces him.*) It's good to be home again, after all!

DEBORAH: " After all " indeed! Did they give you a proper breakfast at the Palace?

JOSEPH: We were all talking so much, I'm afraid I didn't notice.

DEBORAH: Did Pharaoh sit down with you all?

JOSEPH: Yes, and tucked in, too, quite like a human being!

LYSIAS: Rank blasphemy! All the Court set were present, I suppose?

JOSEPH: Old Theocritus arrived about half an hour late, and had to recite a brand new epigram by way of penance. I can't remember a word of it!

DEBORAH: Isn't he looking haggard, poor boy? And no wonder, after all the excitements (*To* JOSEPH.) We got your letter from Antioch. All those awful receptions! And you didn't think you'd be back before Pentecost.

JOSEPH: Once we got down to business, everything went smoothly, thank God.

HELEN: And so you were able to call at Jerusalem on the way back?

JOSEPH: Exactly. (*His voice betrays a kind of grim reserve.*)

DEBORAH: Did you find your grandfather's old house? (*To the visitors.*) My brother and I were born there, you know.

JOSEPH: I found the house. I didn't go inside.

DEBORAH: What did you think of the Temple?

JOSEPH: It didn't come up to my expectations.

DEBORAH: Tell us what else you saw?

HELEN (*as he doesn't answer*): Perhaps he'd like to have a rest now —and talk later. We could come back in an hour or two.

JOSEPH: No, no. Please don't go, any of you. (*To* DEBORAH.) I saw David's Tower and Jeremiah's grotto, and the tombs of the Judges—all the show places. And I made a special excursion to Solomon's Pools, for Uncle Simeon's benefit!

SIMEON (*smiling*): You remembered, eh?

JOSEPH (*abruptly*): But may we talk about all that another time?

DEBORAH (*disappointed*): Aren't you going to tell us anything now?

JOSEPH: Yes, I'm going to tell you—something more important than travellers' gossip, a piece of real news. (*As they stir.*) Something that will be of special interest to Uncle.

SIMEON: To me?

JOSEPH (*slowly*): To you and to seventy-one other learned gentlemen.

LYSIAS: This is all very mystifying.

JOSEPH: It should interest you, too, Lysias—Helen, no less. In fact, it is going to rejoice all seekers after truth, though it may alarm a few faint-hearted brethren!

DEBORAH: Whatever is he coming to?

JOSEPH: Let me begin by explaining that, while it certainly had nothing to do with any trade-agreements, our visit to Jerusalem was by no means a mere pleasure-jaunt. Lysias had an inkling of that, I suspect.

LYSIAS: Our mutual friend at the Library has certainly hinted at mysterious goings on.

JOSEPH: Well, he sponsored the project, so he ought to know! Thanks largely to his enthusiasm (*with controlled emotion*), Pharaoh entrusted me with a personal commission to the High Priest at Jerusalem, as the outcome of which our Holy Writings are to be translated into Greek.

[*There is a general gasp of astonishment.*

DEBORAH: You are not joking?

SIMEON (*in a quavering voice*): I am not dreaming?

JOSEPH: Rather, your dream has come true, Uncle.

SIMEON: I thank the Most High that I have lived to see this day.

JOSEPH: God grant that you may live to see the task of translation carried, with His help, to fruition.

SIMEON (*fervently*): Amen.

JOSEPH: It will be with *your* help, too, Uncle. (SIMEON *starts*.) Yes, yours is among the seventy-two names approved by the High Priest for the great undertaking.

SIMEON: My name? It is not possible! No, no, I am unworthy. . . . (*He breaks down.*) I beg you all to excuse me. . . . (*Quite overcome, he hurries from the room.*)

DEBORAH: He is always so modest. No one would guess what a learned man he is. . . . (*Herself succumbing to her emotions.*) Oh, but, Theophilus! What a triumph! And I haven't even congratulated him yet! I am so proud of you, my boy! (*She embraces him.*)

JOSEPH (*freeing himself*): Thank you, Mother. (*In a rather strained voice.*) I want to ask something of you—of all my friends. I would prefer to be called by my real name in future: my name is Joseph, not Theophilus.

DEBORAH: Your Jewish name, dear.

JOSEPH: I am a Jew, Mother.

DEBORAH (*puzzled*): Just as you wish, my son.

HELEN: Mayn't we call you Theo—I mean, as a pet name?

JOSEPH (*after regarding her*): Yes, I'm talking rather foolishly, aren't I? Of course I'm still " Theo " to all of you. (*Abruptly.*) Let's have some wine, Mother.

DEBORAH (*to her guests*): Nobody's going to decline *that* invitation, I hope!

[*She goes to the sideboard, and during the succeeding speeches transfers from it on to the side-table a jug, some cups, and a plate of cheese biscuits.* Are we allowed to ask questions about your talks in Jerusalem, Theo?

JOSEPH: I won't guarantee to answer.

DEBORAH: You must have had a good many difficulties to overcome.

JOSEPH: It wasn't easy going.

DEBORAH: Did the High Priest receive you all alone? (*She begins to pour out the wine.*)

JOSEPH: In the early stages.

DEBORAH: How did you like him?

JOSEPH: Not much, I'm afraid.

DEBORAH: Was he ungracious to you? . . . Hand round the cups, dear, will you?

JOSEPH (*obeying*) : Oh, he was gracious enough—to Pharaoh's representative ! I think I preferred the rough tongues on the Council !

DEBORAH : Who'll have a biscuit ? (*She circulates the plate.*)

HELEN (*raising her cup*) : Pharaoh's Ambassador ! Joseph ! (*They drink.*)

JOSEPH : And I give you the Seventy-two ! God help them ! (*They drink again.*)

LYSIAS : They'll want some keeping in order, won't they, Theo ? Isn't there a danger of too many cooks spoiling the broth ?

JOSEPH : You might add that most of the cooks are notoriously fond of a good argument ! (*Munching a biscuit.*) The intention, of course, is to minimize the risk of errors in interpretation.

LYSIAS : By sharing out the responsibility ? Safety in numbers !

JOSEPH : Exactly. Our panel will include every Greek-speaking Rabbi of true vocation. The organization, I grant, will be a thorny problem. Fortunately, that won't be my responsibility. (*He sits down suddenly, and buries his head in his hands.*)

HELEN (*signalling her brother*) : We'll leave you now—to a well-earned rest.

JOSEPH (*looking up*) : No. Please don't go yet, Helen.

DEBORAH : You'll stay—both of you—and have a meal ?

LYSIAS (*replacing his cup*) : Thank you, madam, but I am already long overdue at the Library. (*To* JOSEPH.) The great news will be made public during the day, I presume ?

JOSEPH : You will find it has reached the Library ahead of you, I'm afraid. Apollonius was at the breakfast.

LYSIAS : Confound him for that ! (*Moving towards the door.*)

DEBORAH : Do come back later, if you can.

LYSIAS : May we leave it open ? If I can, it will be a pleasure. (*With a bow.*) Compliments to all !

JOSEPH : I'll see you as far as the corner.

[*Murmured leave-taking as the two men withdraw from the scene.*

HELEN : Are you quite sure I'm not in the way ?

DEBORAH : Quite, quite sure ! And you'd like to stay and talk to Theo, I know. . . . (*She motions her back to the couch.*)

HELEN (*seated*) : How much else do you know, I wonder ? (DEBORAH *smiles.*) Did Theo tell you anything before he left ?

43

DEBORAH: Yes, Helen. (*She sits on the couch beside her.*) He told me that he had asked you to be his wife, and that you hadn't been able to make up your mind.

HELEN: Were you angry?

DEBORAH: *Angry* with you—for not deciding an all-important matter in haste?

HELEN: Angry with Theo, I meant—for proposing marriage . . .?

DEBORAH: How can you ask that, my dear? Surely you know, Helen, that Theo couldn't have chosen anyone more dear to me.

HELEN (*drawing closer to her*): You've always made me feel so at home! Ever since that day Theo first brought me here—a total stranger——

DEBORAH: Aged five—crying for her parents!

HELEN: The day of the great Festival! Shall I ever forget it? Those awful, surging crowds, and the cavalry clattering down the street! And the sense of helplessness when Daddy's hand was wrenched out of mine . . . And after that (*she covers her eyes*) . . . until someone picked me up, and then—oh the comfort of Theo's strong arms, and his quiet voice!

DEBORAH: Do you remember how he insisted on going out again at once to let your parents know you were safe? Theo at twelve!

HELEN: He's always been the same in my eyes. I shall always look up to him.

DEBORAH: And yet you hesitated? Like a sensible person!

HELEN: I'd like to tell you why I hesitated . . . (*She pauses.*)

DEBORAH: And you hesitate even now—to tell me! (*Taking her hand.*) I know, my dear!

HELEN (*with a burst*): What nonsense it is to say you're stand-offish—that you don't welcome strangers into your families!

DEBORAH: No, that isn't nonsense, Helen. There's a great deal of truth in it, I'm afraid.

HELEN: Is it because of our worshipping more than one God?

DEBORAH: Chiefly on that account.

HELEN: That was what I wanted to think about before I gave Theo my answer. (*Choosing her words carefully.*) All my life one god and one goddess have been especially real to me: Serapis—as we call him here in Alexandria—and Isis, the Great Mother. . . . Would you call that idolatry?

DEBORAH: Some people would. (*Grimly.*) And if words have power, that's a word to scare Jews with!

HELEN: Yes . . . But I must be absolutely honest about this. Serapis and Isis are real to me—both of them.

DEBORAH: Because you were taught as a child to worship them—or their images——

HELEN: No, no—that isn't the reason. To people who worship them just because they were taught to do so, I don't think they are real at all. With me—I want so badly to make this clear to you, but it's difficult to put into words. . . . (*She pauses before continuing.*) Whenever anything beautifully right and big happens —deep down in me I feel, " There, that was Serapis ! " . . . And in the same way, if I'm feeling desperately sorry for someone—a child, perhaps, or a badly-treated slave—I just find myself praying, inwardly—not to Serapis, but to Isis—Isis the Merciful. . . . Do you despise me for that ?

DEBORAH: How could I, my dear ?

HELEN: I want to tell you that I have been trying to think sincerely about all these things, and about what Theo has told me of your ideas and beliefs. . . . It may sound very foolish to you, but it seems to me that what I have been accustomed to call Serapis and Isis may be—just, as it were, two different faces of the same one supreme God that your people worship. . . . Is that possible, do you think ?

DEBORAH: I'm not clever enough to answer that. But, instead, I'd like to tell you something about myself that you'll think much sillier. When we first came to Alex—and for years and years afterwards—I had a horror of cats . . . not a fear, but a horror— because I'd been told the Egyptians worshipped them. And all Egyptians were idolators. Your mother once offered me a beautiful Persian kitten, and I couldn't bring myself to accept the gift, though I was ashamed to tell her the true reason. And then— years later—you must have often heard me tell the story—a stray cat walked into my bedroom one night, hungry and bedraggled and covered with lice . . . and yet with such dignity and condescension—as though he weren't quite sure he wanted to stay ! And how we had to coax him !

HELEN (*laughing*): You needn't tell me any more ! I know how everybody in this household worships dear Tobias !

DEBORAH (*laughing with her*): And perhaps one oughtn't to be joking over such a serious question. But what I really wanted to say is that I think one ought to judge people by their natures and their behaviour—not by what one has been told of their beliefs.

HELEN: What a difference it would make ! Perhaps we should all come to live together like one great family . . . instead of—as even here in Alex—Egyptians and Jews and Greeks all dividing into their separate quarters. It seems so unfriendly.

DEBORAH: Well, at least it hasn't prevented our two families from becoming friends.

HELEN: And you think it needn't prevent my marrying Theo ?

DEBORAH: If you won't mind moving into this part of the city.

HELEN: Why ever should I ? It's just as nice as ours.

DEBORAH: To tell you the truth, my dear, we think it rather nicer ! And your father won't object ?

HELEN: Not he ! You know how he's always admired Theo—and you as well.

DEBORAH: So you *have* made up your mind—and you won't keep Theo waiting any longer.

HELEN: Theo—Joseph—he's such a fine person, isn't he ?

DEBORAH (*embracing her*): And I think he's a very *lucky* person !

[JOSEPH *re-enters at that moment.*

Ah, there you are, Theo, at last.

JOSEPH: Lysias insisted on my walking him back to the Library. I'm glad you've kept Helen. (*He throws himself on to a chair.*) Yes, it's good to be home again ! (*He reflects.*) Home ! That queer, intangible reality. . . . What *is* home ?

HELEN: Where one's mother is.

DEBORAH: Where one's children will be. (*She rises, and moves to the door.*) No, home is anywhere in God's kingdom. (*She stoops and kisses his forehead in passing.*) I'm going to leave you two now.

[*She goes out. There is a longish silence.*

HELEN: Perhaps you don't want to talk just yet ?

JOSEPH: Oh yes, I want to talk. And to talk to you. (*He rises and begins to pace.*) Where to begin ?

HELEN: Shall *I* begin ?—where we left off last time.

JOSEPH: All those ages ago !

HELEN (*quickly*): Things have changed, you mean ?

JOSEPH: In many ways. (*As she winces.*) I don't love you any less.

HELEN: I am glad. (*A pause.*) I've been afraid at times. . . . I had a silly dream. . . . (*Abruptly.*) Please, I would like to kiss you, Theo.

JOSEPH (*as if suddenly aware of her*): Helen !

HELEN (*in his arms*): I dreamt you had met someone you liked better. . . .

JOSEPH: Dearest ! (*Holding her close.*) *You* haven't changed.

HELEN: Yes, I have. I love you so much—so *very* much more, Theo. (*As he releases her.*) Will you take me to your Synagogue, so that I can be made a Proselyte ?

JOSEPH: You feel quite sure you want to ?

HELEN: Yes. And I want to learn the language of your Scriptures —though I'm glad I shall be able to read them soon in Greek.

JOSEPH: Hardly " soon," I'm afraid. The translation may take years.

HELEN: Then we won't wait for it to get married ! (*He doesn't seem to hear.*) Theo, how soon can the marriage take place ?

JOSEPH: What ? Marriage ? I don't know—I haven't enquired. . . . (*His voice trails away.*)

HELEN: Theo ! Joseph ! Something's wrong. The truth, *please*.

JOSEPH: Yes. That at least ! I ought to have told you at once . . . Helen, I want to go back there—to Judea.

HELEN: But why shouldn't you ? Surely you're not afraid I'd want to keep you always at home ?

JOSEPH: You'll think what I'm going to say quite mad. I want to go to Jerusalem—to live—and die there.

HELEN (*recoiling*): To *live* ? In Jerusalem ? What will you do there ?

JOSEPH: I don't know. I thought of training to become a scribe.

HELEN: A scribe ?

JOSEPH: A fellow who scribbles—copies, if you like—from musty old manuscript—copies, and corrects, and re-edits——

HELEN: But—all your interests here ? Your career ?

JOSEPH: That doesn't amount to much, anyway. Managing the family estates—amassing more money than anyone should be allowed to possess ! Eventually, I suppose, I might be made head of the Jewish Corporation. My work for Pharaoh could never lead anywhere.

HELEN: Why not ?

JOSEPH: Because to hold any permanent office I should have to worship the city gods—a thing no Jew will ever do. . . . Once that was a grievance. Now it all means nothing. Jerusalem means everything.

HELEN: Is it such a beautiful city ?

JOSEPH: No. Compared with Alex, it's a hole—badly planned, shoddily built, dirty, insanitary, drab. Its people are mostly ugly and ill-mannered. And probably it'll be reduced to ashes in the next war with Syria.

HELEN (*bewildered*): Theo !

JOSEPH: Naturally, I couldn't expect you to share a madman's whim. (*Stiffly.*) So I ask to be released from our engagement.

HELEN (*faintly*): There was no engagement on either side. . . . But I would like to understand. . . . Won't you help me ?

JOSEPH: I can't, Helen. I don't understand myself. (*He sits down and stares before him.*) It's the sheerest lunacy ! There's no word in the Greek language for it !

[*He buries his head in his hands.* HELEN *drops into a chair at the other side of the room, and begins to weep silently.* SIMEON *enters, and goes to the table.*

SIMEON: Is there some trouble ?

JOSEPH: Yes. (*He rises.*) I want to go back to Jerusalem—to make my home there.

SIMEON: I can well understand that. (*Softly, to himself.*) " . . . When we remembered Zion . . . " (*He resumes his old seat.*) Helen would understand not so well perhaps.

HELEN (*looking up*): Please, will you teach me to understand ? Theo says he can't. I want to marry him.

SIMEON: I am sorry.

HELEN: You disapprove ?

SIMEON: No, I did not say that. You are very sympathetic to me. I wish only peace for you, as for Joseph.

HELEN: And you think there would be no peace in our marriage ?

SIMEON: You would find it strange in Jerusalem.

JOSEPH: It's out of the question !

HELEN (*turning on him*): Why do you say that ? How can you know ? You must see that I love you with my whole heart. You say that you love me. Isn't that enough ?

SIMEON (*gently*): For Plato it would be enough.

JOSEPH: And for Esdras it would be an abomination !

HELEN: Esdras ? Who was Esdras, please ?

SIMEON: Esdras was a scribe.

HELEN: Oh, a copyist.

SIMEON (*gravely*): A man learned in Torah, strict in observance of the letter, worthy to *write*.

JOSEPH (*with a laugh*): A man who writes over and over again what others have written before. And is honoured for it by the whole population ! A nation of madmen !

HELEN: Please, Theo. (*To* SIMEON.) Be patient with me, Rabbi. Only *teach* me. . . . First, concerning our marriage. This Esdras, this man worthy to write——

SIMEON: But Esdras the scribe did more than write. He found the people who had returned from the Babylonian captivity demoralized by the evil practices of neighbouring tribes. He built up the spirit of the people as surely as others rebuilt the walls of the city. He breathed life into dead bones.

HELEN: He was a strong man, a hero, then. But Theo says he would have abominated our marriage.

SIMEON: He ordered every man who had married a strange woman to put his wife away.

HELEN: That was cruel !

SIMEON: He saved Israel.

HELEN: Yes, I think I see what you mean. (*She thinks hard before continuing.*) The people had become demoralized, you said, by evil practices. What sort of practices ?

SIMEON: Idolatry.

HELEN: Idolatry. Yes, I understand. I suppose the women they had married belonged to idolatrous tribes ?

SIMEON: Barbarians, you would have called them.

HELEN: So it was because they were leading their menfolk into idolatry that these strange women had to be removed ?

SIMEON: Undoubtedly.

HELEN: Am I a barbarian ? If not, what bearing has Esdras on the question of my marrying Theo ?

SIMEON: According to the reasoning of your Socrates, my dear, no bearing whatever. Smaller minds in Jerusalem, unfortunately, would reason otherwise. For them, even as Moses led the nation out of the wilderness, Esdras led it out of the sin of idolatry. Therefore they cling to the letter of his decree, as to the law of Moses.

HELEN: Are the scribes also lawgivers ?

SIMEON: No. Only Moses was the lawgiver.

HELEN: Then Esdras's law has no validity. Unless—— Oh, but it's all so muddling !

[*She begins to weep again.* DEBORAH *returns.*

DEBORAH: Helen in tears ? (*Going to her.*) What has been happening ?

HELEN: What I feared. I am a "strange woman." They won't accept me.

DEBORAH: Who won't ?

HELEN: Esdras, who came from Babylon after the Captivity—and probably Moses as well. . . . It doesn't seem to matter whether a thing's right or wrong. It's how the people in Jerusalem would think someone who lived hundreds of years ago might have thought about something quite different. . . .

DEBORAH: So that's it ! Simeon ! *Did* Moses condemn mixed marriages ?

SIMEON: Mosaic law is silent on the subject.

DEBORAH: As Moses himself married a strange woman, that isn't surprising ! (*Looking round.*) Does anyone here think that Helen isn't good enough for Theo ?

HELEN: No, please, they didn't mean it like that. And no one's accused me of idolatry. . . . All the same, oh I do feel sorry for those poor women condemned without even a chance to prove they were innocent. . . . And I wonder if all the husbands obeyed the order.

SIMEON (*rather grimly*): So far as is known to us.

HELEN: And no one protested ?

DEBORAH: One person at least protested.

JOSEPH: Who was that, Mother ? There's nothing in the Books——

DEBORAH: Perhaps you haven't read all the Books, my son. A Book was once written to vindicate strange women who married Jews. . . . Your uncle will know.

SIMEON: I haven't forgotten.

DEBORAH: As though anyone could forget. . . . (*To the others.*) Our grandfather used to have a special treat for us, when we were small children in Jerusalem. He'd creep into our room, and fetch us downstairs, after everyone else had gone to bed. Then he'd bring the book out from its hiding-place, and swear us to secrecy. And then he'd read us the story of Ruth. . . .

SIMEON: And after that we would have to take the oath again !

DEBORAH: Never to tell anyone in Jerusalem. . . . Well, this isn't Jerusalem ! And Theo has never heard the story of Ruth the Moabitess.

JOSEPH: Never, Mother.

DEBORAH (to HELEN): The Moabites, you must know, are the lowest of all the low tribes surrounding Judea. . . . I'm not going to tell you the story now, but, in the end, Ruth, the strange woman, found a Jewish husband whose name was Boaz, and they had a son whose name was Jesse, and Jesse had a son called David.

HELEN: David—not the great king?

DEBORAH: Yes, the great king himself.

JOSEPH: The Book was kept hidden, you say?

SIMEON: And I think I can tell you the reason. From my researches, it seems that the Book, written shortly after the death of Esdras, provoked so much controversy that the High Priest ordered all copies to be confiscated. A few would no doubt have been preserved surreptitiously, but the order has never been revoked to this day.

DEBORAH: What a pity they are so narrow-minded in Jerusalem! (JOSEPH turns away, biting his lip. An uncomfortable silence.) Have I said something tactless?

JOSEPH: I am going to live in Jerualem.

DEBORAH: Why, my son?

JOSEPH: Because I feel I can serve there.

DEBORAH: Can't you serve here in Alexandria? (He shakes his head.) Why not?

[He drops despairingly into a chair.

HELEN: May I try to answer that question? (He turns to her with a start.) It won't be the right answer perhaps. Theo will correct me in that case. Only I must understand what is in his mind. . . . (Plunging, with desperate eagerness.) In fulfilment of a Promise from God, your nation entered the land of Judea—" our land," Rabbi Simeon called it—more than a thousand years ago. God had given you the land, and in return you—or your fathers— owed Him special service. . . . It was a sort of bargain. Is that right so far?

SIMEON: Yes, it was a covenant.

HELEN: A covenant. And your Torah—including these precious Books that seventy of your scholars are now going to give to us Greeks—and that, I suppose, could only have been written in your own land——? (Looking enquiringly towards SIMEON.)

SIMEON: Yes, they were part of the bargain, we believe.

HELEN: Perhaps Theo believes that that isn't the end of the bargain. . . . Perhaps he thinks it's only a kind of instalment. Perhaps he thinks the work in the land of the Covenant is to go on for ever and ever.

DEBORAH: Is that the right answer, Theo?

JOSEPH (*hopelessly*): Perhaps.

HELEN: Or perhaps—perhaps—— (*Turning to* JOSEPH.) Theo, you told me once about a hope revealed through your Prophets that a new kind of king would one day come into the world. You called him by a special name. What was the word?

JOSEPH (*tonelessly*): Messias.

HELEN: Theo, does the hope of Messias belong to the work of the Covenant?

JOSEPH (*with a shrug*): It may be so. (*Relapsing into his former listlessness.*) I don't know. . . . It's no good. I don't know anything. (*He rises.*) I can tell you only what happened to me—that day—just outside Jerusalem. (*He is gazing into space.*)

DEBORAH: Wait! I hear someone coming.

[LYSIAS *returns in a state of some excitement.*

LYSIAS (*looking round*): All present! Excellent! (*Addressing* DEBORAH.) Returning at your invitation, madam, I bring with me a tit-bit of gossip to pay for my welcome! A mere whisper at present, it comes, I can assure you, from an unimpeachable source—straight from the Palace stables, as you might say! Our Theo, ladies and gentlemen, is to receive an honour unprecedented in Egyptian history!

DEBORAH (*murmuring politely*): That is gratifying. . . .

LYSIAS (*his eyes on* JOSEPH): To your son no less than to you, I trust, madam! (*Approaching him.*) Pharaoh, it seems, is in ecstasies over the success of your negotiations, Theo. He is already planning an elaborate Academy to accommodate the Seventy on Pharos Island. He has also been wrestling with the problem of suitably recognizing your services. (JOSEPH *makes a gesture.*) Oh, he is alive to your scruples, and insistent that they shall be respected. And so, with typical ingenuity, he has devised a new order of what is to be called " honorary citizenship." In short, you are to be offered a Court appointment, coupled with the gift of the freedom of the city of Alexandria! (*In the silence that follows.*) Is nobody here disposed to show the slightest interest in my information?

HELEN (*quietly*): Theo will decline both the gift and the offer, Lysias.

LYSIAS (*thunderstruck*): What? (*Bewildered.*) Will someone kindly enlighten me?

HELEN: Theo is leaving Alexandria—for ever.

LYSIAS: Leaving——? Where is he going to?

HELEN: To the Holy City of the Jews.

LYSIAS (*weighing this*): Is it so? (*Regarding* SIMEON.) The Rabbi was right, then. (*Turning to* HELEN.) But—Helen—what about your——? (*He checks himself.*)

HELEN (*to the others*): Lysias knew that Theo had asked me to marry him. (*To* LYSIAS.) That is a separate question. (*To* JOSEPH.) Theo, before Lysias came in, you were going to tell us of something that happened to you. Please go on.

JOSEPH: There's nothing much to tell. And it doesn't make sense. It was only the way it affected me. . . . It'll bore Lysias.

HELEN: Never mind that.

JOSEPH (*as it were, in the witness-box*): It was on the second day of Passover. I had spent Seder night at the High Priest's house, and the next morning I attended the service in the Temple, but left in the middle. I was hating Jerusalem, and everybody in it, and hating myself into the bargain. I thought I would go for a long walk and try to clear my mind. I don't remember by which road I left the city, or how long I'd been walking, but on my way back, I was in sight of the Damascus Gate, when I suddenly stopped dead. . . . The thing that stopped me was the recollection of some lines from the Prophet Esaias. They seemed to drop on to my tongue—I can't describe it in any other way. I found myself repeating the lines over and over again. . . .

> " He hath no form nor comeliness that we should
>   look upon him.
> Nor beauty that we should desire him.
> He is despised and rejected of men.
> A man of sorrows and acquainted with grief;
> And as one from whom men hide their faces he
>   was despised;
> And we esteemed him not."

(*He passes his hand over his brow.*) I can't go on. Sorry. That's all. (*He turns away.*)

HELEN: The Prophet Esaias—who was he referring to?

JOSEPH: Nobody knows. It might be every Jew. Esaias calls him simply the Lord's servant. It's a mystery. I have no theories on the subject. I know only the effect of those words upon me at that spot—it was on a slope called Golgotha, which means the place of a skull—and it was about the ninth hour of the day. . . . (*He breaks off.*) I only know—I only know——

LYSAIS (*after an uncomfortable silence*): Well, I must say——

HELEN: No, please, Lysias !

LYSIAS: I'm sorry, but I think it's pretty rough on you, Helen. And I suggest it's time we both left this house.

HELEN: Do you go, Lysias, by all means. I am staying on. There is something I have to say to Theo. (LYSIAS, *with compressed lips, walks straight out.*) This is what I want to say. (DEBORAH *and* SIMEON *exchange glances.*) I want to say it to all of you, please. If Theo's place is in Jerusalem, my place is by his side. If life has to be difficult there, the more reason for me to share it with him. Theo (*turning to him*), you say the meaning of these happenings is not clear to you. Perhaps Messias when he comes will make all things clear. Perhaps only Messias can make clear why I know with certainty that your people are my people, and your God my God.

[JOSEPH *does not move.*

DEBORAH: One thing you will have to do in Jerusalem, my son.

JOSEPH: What is that, Mother ?

DEBORAH: Publish the Book of Ruth.

JOSEPH: I will write it again, if necessary. (*He takes* HELEN *in his arms.*)

[SIMEON *raises his hands in benediction.*

CURTAIN

NOTE

Alexandria was founded in 331 B.C. Ptolemy II, known as Philadelphus, came to the throne of Egypt in 285, and reigned till his death in 246. In 277 he married his sister, Arsinoe II, who died in 270; between these years Theocritus wrote his fifteenth Idyll, describing Alexandrian street scenes during an Adonis Festival, which suggested the occasion on which " boy meets girl " for my purposes. The Septuagint, so far as we know, might have been commenced any time between 285 and 247. The characters projected against this background are fictitious, except Tobias, whose acquaintance I made while writing a not very amusing play.

OHAD'S WOMAN

" So he cometh to a city of Samaria called Sychar . . . and Jacob's well was there. Jesus therefore being wearied with his journey sat thus by the well. It was about the sixth hour. There cometh a woman of Samaria to draw water. Jesus saith unto her, Give me to drink. For his disciples were gone away into the city to buy food. . . .

And upon this came his disciples; and they marvelled that he was speaking with a woman. . . . So the woman left her waterpot and went away into the city. . . . In the meanwhile the disciples prayed him, saying, Rabbi, eat. But he said unto them, I have meat to eat that ye know not. . . . Lift up your eyes, and look on the fields that they are white already unto harvest."—St. John, Chapter IV.

CHARACTERS

OHAD
KENAZ
NAARAH } Samaritans
POL

MATTHEW, a Jew

Scene: Back garden of a house in Shechem (or Sychar), Samaria
Time: Morning in the early summer of A.D. 27

A low hedge separates the garden from a lane, sloping down from left to right of the spectator, along the background of the scene. There is a gate (or gap) in the middle. The back entrance to the house, which need not be visible, is on the right. In the shade of a palm-tree, OHAD, the householder, a squat, paunchy, but sturdy, bearded, middle-aged intellectual, is reclining on a divan. Beside him is a table from which he can reach a flagon of wine and a goblet. Beyond the table is a garden seat. OHAD has been reading, and all about him are strewn expanded scrolls of parchment. Now he is dozing, and presently he emits a snore. KENAZ, a tall, well-preserved, prosperous-looking man of the same generation, strolling down the lane, sees him, stops and calls familiarly.

KENAZ: My neighbour Ohad is not receiving visitors this morning!

OHAD (*bestirring himself*): What's that? (*Looking up.*) Kenaz! Come in and have a drink!

KENAZ: And disturb a good man at his meditations?

OHAD: Come in at once, I say! (*Calling across to the house.*) Naarah! More wine—and a cup for Kenaz! (KENAZ *enters the garden through the gate.*) What do you think of this heat? And why do you never come to see me nowadays, you old scoundrel?

KENAZ: Do you ever come and see me, may I ask?

OHAD: I'm a busy man—not a gentleman of leisure, like you. (KENAZ *seats himself on the bench.*) Naarah! Some more wine! Wine for the company!

NAARAH (*off, in an even voice*): I heard you the first time, dear.

KENAZ: Naarah keeps you well, I see. She is keeping well herself, I trust?

57

OHAD: Oh, Naarah's always fit. How's that little what's-her-name of yours?

KENAZ: Sherah? Increasing in size, but not in intelligence. I regret to say. (*Enter* NAARAH *with another flagon and cup. She is a small person, pale with deep-set eyes and a great shock of hair. She is humming softly to herself.*) Greeting, Naarahkins! (*She deposits the wine and cup on the table.*)

OHAD: Thank you, my pet. Have some yourself.

NAARAH: Not now. I'm in the middle of cooking dinner. (*She pours out for* KENAZ.) Would I have kept Kenaz waiting for anything less imperative? (*She brings* KENAZ *his cup.*)

KENAZ (*taking it from her*): And a kiss for old acquaintance?

[*She bends down, and their lips meet. She returns to pour out for* OHAD.

NAARAH: You might have brought Sherah with you.

OHAD (*as she hands him his cup*): Leave it on the table, will you? (*He pats her cheek as she complies.*)

KENAZ: That reminds me. Sherah says if you don't come and help her with her spring-cleaning she's going to have a nervous breakdown!

NAARAH: I'll drop in one day next week, tell her. (*Remembering.*) My cooking! (*As she turns to go.*) Don't let him go too soon, Ohad!

[OHAD, *who is engaged in reading one of his scrolls, grunts non-committally. She returns to the house.* KENAZ *sips his wine contentedly.*

KENAZ (*presently*): What's the book, Ohad?

OHAD: It's a new edition of the Prophet Isaiah. Amazing fellow! Listen to this (*reading*): " He was oppressed, yet he humbled himself, and opened not his mouth; as a lamb is led to the slaughter, and as a sheep before her shearers is dumb, so he opened not his mouth. He was taken away without justice: and who cared how he fell? For he was cut off out of the land of the living."

KENAZ: What does it all mean?

OHAD: Oh, the meaning doesn't matter so much. It's probably the old Redeemer of Israel idea seen from a new angle. But the style! You and I couldn't write like that.

KENAZ (*after a short pause*): I have long suspected my friend Ohad of a secret hankering after these good old Judaic superstitions?

OHAD: Well, there's Judaic blood in my veins. . . .

KENAZ: Naturally. (*With a laugh.*) Considering the known facts of history, it's an extraordinary thing that I seem to be the only inhabitant of Samaria who doesn't claim kinship with our arrogant and detestable neighbours.

OHAD: Very well, then. Leaving my genealogy out of the question, I confess I find this Messianic theory an attractive speculation.

KENAZ: I see no attraction in any speculation.

OHAD: The country's in a bloody awful state. You can see that, I suppose?

KENAZ: You and I can do nothing about it—so why worry?

OHAD: We're involved.

KENAZ: Are we? I haven't noticed it. . . . Seriously, I don't see what a man can do with his life—even a man of means and position—beyond cultivating his personality and making a woman or two happy for a year or two apiece.

OHAD: And with his money? He's to shut his eyes, of course, to everything that goes on outside his immediate social circle?

KENAZ: Not in the least. He can serve the community as you and I do—sit on a hundred and one committees.

OHAD: Yes, all that's very consoling, isn't it? Unfortunately, it doesn't suffice to prevent one feeling damnably depressed at times.

KENAZ: What's the matter with you, old chap? Been having a row with Naarah?

OHAD: Funny you should say that. Naarah has a theory that whenever I start carrying on about the state of the world it only means I'm annoyed with her about something. Not that we ever have any real rows.

KENAZ: No. One doesn't—with Naarah. But it's annoying when a woman's charms begin to pall—as, sooner or later, every woman's must——

OHAD: I shall always have a deep affection for Naarah. There's no one like her. (*He pauses.*)

KENAZ: You're more interested in somebody else, I expect?

OHAD: That's all there is to it.

KENAZ: Naarah's a sensible girl. She won't give you any trouble.

OHAD: If only she weren't in love with me. There are two states of acute misery that it seems to me a man just has to grind his teeth and put up with: one is being in love with a woman, who isn't to be had on any terms; the other is not being in love with a woman and feeling that her whole life has been blighted in consequence. . . . Of the two, I suppose the latter is the less disagreeable. . . . Still, when you are very fond of the woman—as I am of Naarah—it isn't pleasant to see yourself making her suffer.

KENAZ: Would you like me to speak to her. I might be able to help in straightening things out.

OHAD: It'll come to the same thing in the end. There's no way round these torturing situations. Sooner or later the thing has to come to a crisis—confound it !

[NAARAH re-appears from the house, followed by POL, a pretty girl of eighteen.

NAARAH: Here's another visitor come to cheer you up, Ohad.

POL: I do like that ! I come all this way to have a heart to heart talk with Naarah about the problem of my new frock, and before I can say Nebuchadnezzar she drags me out here, and wants to fob me off on to Ohad ! (NAARAH has returned to the house.) And now she's disappeared again !

OHAD (brightening up): Naarah has better things to do with her time than to gossip with young chits like you ! Sit down and make yourself sociable. (Calling.) Naarah ! Another cup for the company ! (NAARAH arrives with it as he speaks.) You know Kenaz ?

POL: Who doesn't know Kenaz ! (NAARAH has poured out and hands her a cup.) Thanks, darling. (To OHAD.) I suppose you'd never think of offering your comfortable divan to a visitor ? (NAARAH has slipped back into the house.)

OHAD: I'll make room for you, if you like. (She grimaces at him. He lifts his glass.) Pretty Pol ! (He drinks.)

POL (copying him with a giggle): Ugly Ohad !

OHAD: I can tell you all you want to know about that new frock of yours.

POL: You ? I don't believe you ever notice how a woman's dressed. I might as well have nothing on at all.

KENAZ: I can see I'm going to be left out of this conversation.

POL: Don't worry ! I'm not going to stay. (She rises.) I've got all my shopping to do. (She turns to go, blowing a kiss to OHAD.)

OHAD: Wait a jiffy ! (He leaps from the divan.) I'll come as far as the market-place with you. (Seizing her arm.) Here, let's take the short cut, and I'll race you down the hill !

[He runs her through the gap in the hedge and off right. KENAZ *stares after them for a moment, then, with a shrug, settles himself in the divan.* NAARAH *joins him almost immediately after.*

NAARAH: Sorry to deprive you of Ohad's company, but it did seem such a heaven-sent opportunity of restoring his spirits !

KENAZ: Have you finished all your kitchen matters ?

NAARAH: I shall have to go for the water presently.

KENAZ: It won't hurt you to sit down for two seconds.

NAARAH: It'll be rather nice ! (*She squats on the ground, facing him.*)

KENAZ: Like old times, eh ?

NAARAH: Don't remind me ! You were my first husband, and that's going back a good many years.

KENAZ: How many have you had since ?

NAARAH: Four or five. I've almost lost count.

KENAZ: I think in many ways I was the most satisfactory of them.

NAARAH (*qualifying this*): In some ways.

KENAZ: I've never quite stopped missing you.

NAARAH: Flattery can be very warming.

KENAZ: Flattery ? I meant it in deadly earnest, as it happens. I'm going to make a proposal for your consideration.

NAARAH (*taken aback*): Kenaz ! Not—surely—you couldn't mean that we should live together again ?

KENAZ: Not on the old terms, of course. All that's long since burned itself out—on both sides, eh ? Besides, dear Sherah, with all her faults—is a very companionable little monkey. She simply adores you, by the way.

NAARAH: We've always got on well together.

KENAZ: Mind you, she can be very trying at times. If only she could control that tongue of hers ! As for her housekeeping deficiencies—the place is beginning to look like a pigsty !

NAARAH: I'll come along and tidy up for you, with pleasure.

KENAZ: It isn't only the tidying up. There are arrears of mending and sewing—and then there's the cooking, of course—and, oh, countless incidental matters. My idea is that one of these days you should just walk in and take over the household for me—Sherah included.

NAARAH: One of these days ?

KENAZ: Quite.

NAARAH: As a sort of housekeeper-friend, you mean ?

KENAZ: I'm asking you to be my wife.

NAARAH: It's very original of you.

KENAZ: A brainwave, my dear. It would be an unconventional *ménage*, I grant you, but then we are all unconventional people. For instance, you and I would never dream of interfering in one another's private affairs. On the other hand, your company, as well as your services, would be simply a godsend to me. And I thought it might amuse you to have a secure background and an official status in society.

NAARAH (*shortly*): Thanks. (*She rises to her feet, thinking hard.*)

KENAZ: There's no need to decide anything in a hurry. I shan't withdraw the offer—in fact, you can look on it as a kind of insurance, in case you should ever find yourself at a loose end. One of these days—who knows?—you may feel you want a change of atmosphere.

NAARAH (*shrewdly*): One of these days, again. . . . Ohad has been telling you, I suppose, that it's all over between us. (*He doesn't answer.*) I've seen it looming over me, of course—ever since Pol came into the picture. I just can't make up my mind what to do about it. It was decent of you to make me that offer, Kenaz. I appreciate it.

KENAZ: Pure selfishness on my part, I assure you.

NAARAH: I've got over these things before now.

KENAZ (*gently*): I fancy none of the others have meant quite so much to you.

NAARAH: Have I been so blatant about it? It's perfectly idiotic of me—(*she is speaking through tears*), but I just can't bear the thought of not ever living with Ohad again. . . . Only please don't tell him so! He hates to be made to feel responsible for another person's happiness. . . . I *am* a fool. (*She weeps unrestrainedly.*)

KENAZ (*gently*): Just let yourself go. It'll do you good.

NAARAH: No, it won't. . . . (*She pulls herself together with an effort.*) I always said it would never happen to me—to love one person so much that none of the others mattered. And now. . . . It serves me right, I suppose, for thinking, I was different from other women. . . . Only I wish—I wish it hadn't been Pol. She won't be any use to him.

KENAZ: Empty-headed, greedy little baggage!

NAARAH: Oh no, she's not at all a bad sort. It's just that she's not *right* for him. Poor kiddy, I shall have such a job with her when she finds she's beginning to get on his nerves. . . . She's so dependent on me.

KENAZ: Aren't you jealous of her?

NAARAH: Jealous? I don't think so. Ought one to be? I'm a bit sore—but not with Pol. How could she help herself? With Ohad perhaps. But one can't blame anyone. These things just happen, don't they?

KENAZ: They happen to me often enough, heaven knows!

NAARAH (*drying her eyes*): How I hate all this business of weeping. It's so degrading. Shake me hard if I break out again, will you, Kenaz?

KENAZ: Why not give my plan a trial?

NAARAH: It wouldn't suit me.

KENAZ: What would? Or, rather, what alternatives are there? One has to look ahead, you know.

NAARAH: I know all that—and I know I'm twenty-eight, and beginning to look it. And I hate to think of myself just degenerating into an evil-tempered old hag.

KENAZ: You'd make a great hit as my wife.

NAARAH: It wouldn't be me. I must just go my own way, with or without company, for as long as I can keep it up.

KENAZ: And after that?

NAARAH: Who knows? What does it matter, anyway? . . . (*She rises.*) You can tell Ohad I shall be clearing out early to-morrow morning. It'll be a weight off his mind, won't it?

KENAZ: You know he's profoundly grateful to you . . . ?

NARRAH: I'll be grateful to him if he'll let me go without any speeches.

KENAZ: Where will you move to?

NAARAH: I don't know. I must get somewhere right away.

KENAZ: Away from Shechem?

NAARAH (*nodding*): I don't think I could ever settle here again. I may go for a long tramp in the hills. . . . My mind is just an arid waste at present.

KENAZ: You'll fall on your feet again before long.

NAARAH: Of course I shall. And now I'm going to turn you out, my dear. I want to clear up all this mess before I go for the water. (*She commences to collect the papers as she speaks.*) Of all my numerous

63

husbands, I can truthfully say that none could compare with Ohad for untidiness ! . . . (*Abruptly.*) I may not see you again. (*She goes to kiss him.*)

KENAZ : If I were the praying sort, my dear——

NAARAH (*lightly*) : I know, bless you—you'd pray that just as soon as I've got this place straight some perfectly irresistible young nobleman—worth all the rest of my male acquaintants put together—should drop straight out of the clouds and fall on his knees before me !

KENAZ (*laughing with her*) : Don't bother to see me out.

[*He goes off into the house. She stands for a moment waving to him, then, humming lightly to herself, returns to her job. Having collected all the books and papers, she carries them carefully into the house, emerging shortly after to clear away the wine vessels. As she disappears with these into the house, a lean, hook-nosed scarecrow of a man enters from the opposite side, panting as he makes his way down the lane. At the gap in the hedge he pauses, resting on his staff, tempted by the sight of a shelter from the sun. At that moment* NAARAH *reappears from the house, bearing a large water-pot on her shoulders. She stares at the stranger who, unconscious of her presence, suddenly drops on his knees in silent prayer.* NAARAH *recoils, then muttering, " My young nobleman ! " bursts out laughing, at which the stranger, visibly disconcerted, rises to his feet and begins to move on his way.*

NAARAH (*arresting him*) : I'm so sorry. I wasn't laughing at you. It was only something that came into my head. You are feeling the heat, I can see. Won't you come in and rest yourself ?

STRANGER (*hesitating*) : You are very kind. . . . Just for a moment perhaps. . . . (*He stumbles through the gap and, lowering her water-pot, she helps him on to the seat.*) Thank you. But I must not tarry. Perhaps you could tell me where I might buy some food ? I have come from Jerusalem.

NAARAH : I don't sell food, but you are welcome to what I can provide.

STRANGER : It is not for myself. . . .

NAARAH : Nonsense. Anyone can see you are half-famished. Too proud, of course ! Such low creatures, aren't we, reverend master ?

STRANGER : I am not a Rabbi.

NAARAH : Master Levi, then.

STRANGER (*with a wry smile*) : My name used to be Levi, as it happens.

NAARAH: Used to be?

STRANGER: Now it is Matthew. I'm sorry you should think me proud. I assure you no creature could be lower than I have been.

NAARAH: You are a reformed character, I suppose? (*Sitting beside him.*) What was your particular form of crime?

MATTHEW: I used to spend my day sitting behind a counter in an office, screwing money out of poor people, under the protection of an armed Roman guard.

NAARAH: Oh, you were a Publican?

MATTHEW: Levi was a Publican. Matthew is something quite different, something new, a kind of experiment. . . . I wonder if you can understand what I'm talking about.

NAARAH: You are certainly a very odd sort of Jew, but, like all Jews, you are wanting to preach. I can see it in your eye.

MATTHEW: I am not worthy to preach—not at present.

NAARAH: Then I hope you'll resist the temptation. . . . (*As he remains silent.*) You mustn't mind my teasing you. I tease everyone. It's just a habit of mine.

MATTHEW (*earnestly*): I wanted to tell you what happened to me.

NAARAH: Happened to Levi the Publican, you mean?

MATTHEW: Yes. That isn't preaching surely—just telling what happened. My old life was so evil, and it seems so wonderful to have escaped from it. I had inherited the business from my father, you see: I seemed to belong to it. And the more money I made, the more my thirst for it increased—it had enslaved me! And all the time, secretly, I was hating myself, as I hated everybody and everything around me. . . . Hate, hate, hate! Can you imagine what it was like?

NARRAH: No. I don't think I've ever hated anyone.

MATTHEW: Your life has been blessed.

NAARAH (*involuntarily betraying her inner state*): That's interesting news!

MATTHEW (*looking at her*): You are unhappy. I could see that from the first.

NAARAH: We were discussing your case—not mine.

MATTHEW: Yes. It was as if I were doomed to perpetual imprisonment. And now I am a free man.

NAARAH: You decided to throw up the business?

MATTHEW: Not I. By myself I could never have decided anything. Levi the Publican was too strong in me. I was set free (*impressively*) in just two words spoken by another.

NAARAH: By your wife, I suppose?

MATTHEW: No. It was some one sent by God. " Follow me," he said. That was all.

NAARAH: That kind of talk is rather wasted on me, I'm afraid. It isn't only that I don't believe in your God.

MATTHEW: Oh.

NAARAH: I don't *want* to believe in him. The truth is, I hate the very idea of a God who prowls around on the look out for people sufficiently miserable and desperate to be bribed by his pity into worshipping him. I prefer to depend on myself.

MATTHEW: You can't always.

NAARAH: At least I can steer clear of this God of yours.

MATTHEW: Don't be too sure of that either. (*He rises.*) I have been keeping you. I feel much better now.

NAARAH: You will find a baker at the last house but one at the bottom of the hill. Tell him Ohad's woman sent you. He'll do anything for me.

MATTHEW: I am grateful. (NAARAH *shoulders her water-pot.*) You are going to fetch the household water?

NAARAH: From a well at the top of the hill. Jacob's well we call it. You must have passed it on your way down.

MATTHEW: Yes. I noticed a well. . . . (*Abruptly.*) I will bid you good day. (*He turns to go.*)

NAARAH: Well, good luck to you!

[*She motions him before her, and he inclines his head, preoccupied in silent prayer. Passing out of the garden before her, he turns away and off to the right. She, following him into the lane, goes slowly off in the opposite direction. The stage remains empty for some moments, then voices are heard off, from the house, followed by* POL *in person.*

POL: She's not here. What did I tell you?

[OHAD *and* KENAZ *have arrived on the scene.*

OHAD: She's gone for the water, I expect. She's sure to be back presently.

POL: Well, I'm not going to wait! (*She turns to go.*)

OHAD: Oh, yes, you are! You're going to do exactly what you're told, young woman!

[*He has seized her by the wrists, and forces her on to the seat, after a show of resistance on her part.*

66

POL (*to* KENAZ): Did you ever see such a filthy great bully ! (*To* OHAD.) I'll give Naarah only till the sun reaches the tip of my big toe—not a moment longer ! That is, if Kenaz will wait for her with me. (OHAD *has settled himself in the divan.*)

KENAZ: I'm not waiting for Naarah, anyway. I came back with Ohad because there was something I wanted to tell him.

POL (*jumping up*): That settles it ! I'm in the way.

KENAZ: On the contrary, what I have to say will probably interest you no less than Ohad.

POL: It isn't about Naarah, I suppose ?

KENAZ: Yes.

POL: Does that mean you've guessed ?

KENAZ (*innocently*): Guessed ? Guessed what ? Is there some mystery ?

POL (*coyly*): May I tell him, Ohad ?

OHAD (*closing his eyes*): If you like.

POL: Something wonderful has happened, Kenaz ! Ohad and I have fallen in love.

KENAZ (*with an effort*): How—how very extraordinary !

POL: But I haven't told you the worst. Ohad wants me to come and live with him and *I've refused*. I won't hear of it ! As I keep telling him, I would never *dream* of coming between him and Naarah. How could I—when Naarah's my best friend ? (*With a sigh.*) It's all so difficult !

OHAD: And now—if you'll kindly allow Kenaz to get a word in. . . . (*She pouts.*)

KENAZ: What I have to say may perhaps make matters easier for both of you. Naarah's going away.

POL (*eagerly*): When ?

KENAZ: She's clearing out to-morrow morning.

POL (*joyfully*): Not really ? Ohad !

OHAD: It seems rather unnecessarily precipitate. I think she might have consulted me before making such a drastic decision.

KENAZ: There was nothing really to discuss, was there ? She asked me to say she'd be grateful if you could spare her a farewell scene.

OHAD (*uneasily*): Did she ? (*He gets out of the divan.*)

POL: Ohad ! Aren't you glad ?

OHAD (*genuinely*): I shall miss her very much.

KENAZ: You will, if I may speak from experience.

POL: *I* shall miss her, too.

OHAD: Where is she going to?

KENAZ: She hadn't decided anything.

OHAD (*quickly*): She won't be leaving Shechem, will she?

KENAZ: It seems probable.

OHAD: I don't know how the devil we shall manage without her. How would you like to move in here to-morrow, Pol?

POL: I'd love it! (*Going to him.*) We are going to have such a lovely time together, aren't we? And isn't it lucky that Naarah has decided to go now! Dear Naarah, true to her reputation for never staying long in one place. I expect she's been wanting to go for a long time. But we are so perfectly suited to each other— don't you think we are, Kenaz?

KENAZ: I think—well, at any rate I am in favour of celebrating the occasion.

OHAD: An excellent idea! (*Calling.*) Naarah! Wine for the company!... Dammit, I'd forgotten!

POL: *I* know where she keeps the things. (*She bustles out, blowing him a kiss on the way.*)

OHAD (*showing signs of nervous irritation*): What the devil has she done with all my books and papers?

KENAZ: Put them neatly back in their places, I have no doubt.

OHAD (*pacing restlessly*): Did you notice that horde of beggars standing about in the market square?

KENAZ: I can't say I did.

OHAD: The number of utterly hopeless faces one sees about everywhere nowadays! Things can't go on like this for ever. (*Emphatically.*) There's something rotten in the state of Samaria!

[POL *returns with the wine.*

POL: There! Haven't I been quick about it, too! (*She deposits her tray on the table and proceeds to pour out and hand round as she prattles.*) I shall soon know my way about the house; it's such an easy place to manage. I do think it was clever of you to choose just this house to live in.

OHAD: Naarah chose it for me.

POL: Did she? Of course, you mustn't expect me to be quite as capable and efficient as Naarah.

68

OHAD: We shan't. (*He turns to* KENAZ, *gloomily.*) What's going to become of her, Kenaz?

KENAZ: That's what I'd like to know. (*He shrugs his shoulders.*) Did you realize she was twenty-eight?

POL: What, Naarah? I say, is she really as old as all that? I do feel sorry for her. She's been a good friend to me.

KENAZ: Is there anyone she hasn't been a good friend to, I should like to know? There's something altogether peculiar about Naarah. I believe she's only really happy when she's doing things for other people. It's as though she really cared more for other people than for herself. I don't think I've ever heard her grumble. . . . . And her patience! And her good humour! And her grit!

OHAD (*letting his cup fall*): Is this your idea of celebrating? It sounds to me more like a funeral oration!

POL: I shall begin to howl presently!

KENAZ (*with sudden warmth*): You? What have you got to howl about? You with your youth and your sex appeal and your appetites, and with all the romantic possibilities of a cat-and-dog existence in front of you! Wait till you're Naarah's age—then you may have something to howl about. But Naarah's not howling. She's had her fun, and she's paid for it, and so long as there's another drop to be squeezed out of the cup she'll not let go of it. But she knows that all the wailing and gnashing of teeth will not avail to replenish the cup that has once been drained.

POL: And that's what we shall all come to in the end, I suppose. Gives you something to think about, doesn't it?

OHAD: " Like grass . . . in the morning it flourisheth, and groweth up; in the evening it is cut down, and withereth."

KENAZ: The voice of wisdom—the last word on the subject——

[*Silence falls upon the group.*

POL (*pricking up her ears*): There's some one in a great hurry. (*After investigation.*) It's Naarah!

[*All rise apprehensively as* NAARAH *bursts into the garden, out of breath.*

NAARAH: Ohad! Kenaz! Pol!

OHAD: Whatever's the matter?

KENAZ (*as she struggles for words*): Take it easy, Naarahkins. . . . (*He helps her on to the seat.*)

NAARAH: I've found—I've found—a Man——

POL (*heartily*): Good for you, darling !

KENAZ: A drop to revive you ?

[*She rejects it.*

OHAD: Where have you come from ?

NAARAH (*more calmly*): I was only at the well. I went there for the water.

OHAD: What have you done with the water-pot ?

NAARAH: I must have left it behind.

OHAD: May I ask how you think we are going to manage here without water ?

NAARAH: I shall be going back again presently. (*Half rising.*)

KENAZ: There's no need to hurry, is there ? Anyone with half an eye can see you've had a shock. Just sit quietly for a bit, unless you'd like to try and tell us exactly what happened.

NAARAH: Yes. (*After a pause.*) He was sitting there, resting, though I hardly noticed him till he came up and asked if I'd give him a drink. He had a Jewish accent, so while he was drinking the water I couldn't help having a dig at him. I said, " Fancy you asking a Samaritan to get you a drink. I thought your people would never have anything to do with Samaritans." He smiled and said very seriously, " If you knew what God had to give you and who it was that asked you for water you would have asked him instead, and he would have given you living water to drink." I didn't take him seriously. I said, " Why, you have nothing to draw water with, and this is a deep well. Where is your living water to come from ? You must be a greater man than old Father Jacob, who gave us the well and drank, and gave his own sons and his cattle drink from it ! " He didn't answer at first—just quietly went on drinking. Then he looked straight at me and said —I'm trying to give you his exact words : " Whoever drinks of this water will become thirsty again ; whoever drinks of the water I have to give will never thirst again. The water I give you will become in you a spring of water welling up into Eternal Life."

OHAD (*arrested*): Whatever did he mean by that ?

KENAZ: How they love to juggle with words, these fellows !

NAARAH: I couldn't take it in, either. But I looked at him properly for the first time, and after that I didn't try to be funny again. I said, just stupidly, " Will you give me some of that water, please, so that I don't ever have to come to the well again ? "

70

What do you think he said then? " Go and call your husband and come back to me." I said, " I have no husband." " You speak the truth," he said, " you have had five, and the man you are now living with is not your husband either."

POL: That was pretty cool, I must say.

OHAD: You're not making this up?

NAARAH (*shaking her head*): He knew all about me—as though he could see into my mind. And that made it all so much easier—there was nothing I could hide from him if I'd wanted to. I found myself asking him about things I'd never wanted to discuss with anyone before—things I'd pretended didn't interest me. I asked him if the Jews were right in saying that you couldn't worship God in Samaria, but only in Jerusalem. He said that the worship of God had nothing to do with particular places, but that the time was coming when it would be understood that *really* God could only be worshipped in the spirit and in truth. " God is a spirit," he kept saying.

KENAZ: " And you are a bore," I should have answered.

OHAD: Did he say anything else?

NAARAH (*in a strange voice*): Yes. He said something else.

OHAD: What was it?

NAARAH: It was after I had made some reference to the belief in a Messiah who would be coming to enlighten us about all these matters. He said, " I that am speaking to you am he." (*She pauses.*) I knew at once it was the truth. Then Matthew came up with the others. Matthew—but you don't know him, of course. They are his followers. I can't tell you anything more. You must come and see for yourselves.

POL: What, tramp all the way up to the well in this heat? Have a heart, Naarah dear!

NAARAH (*turning to the men*): What about you two?

KENAZ: I'm going to be brutally frank, Naarahkins—I think you'd prefer me to be.

NAARAH: Of course I would, Kenaz.

KENAZ: It's evident this fellow has made a tremendous impression on you, and I'm quite aware that some of these itinerant magicians, with their queer jargon, and their tricks and their mystifications, can be extraordinarily plausible. But one mustn't take them seriously—they're all bogus, just so many mountebanks. In fact, a regular pest. Ohad will bear me out: anyone who's travelled in Judea knows all about them. . . . I hate to hurt your feelings, my dear——

NAARAH: You needn't worry about my feelings—or about hurting me—any of you—any more. All that belongs to the old life—to a part of me which wasn't real. Something in me that I didn't know existed has come up in its place. Something that can't die. It's all that I need. (*She waits a moment.*) Well, I've done what he asked me to do. I'm going back to him now. (*She turns away and walks slowly out, left, amid silence.*)

POL (*awed*): Has she gone batty? Naarah of all people—— If there's one thing I admired about her it was her common sense. You always knew where you were with Naarah. And now—to hear her spouting all that tosh——

KENAZ: I shouldn't wonder if the whole thing weren't a figment of her imagination. One has heard of such cases before—perfectly strong-minded people, under stress of some emotional upheaval, succumbing to the most fantastic hallucinations. . . . What do you think, Ohad?

OHAD: I think—(*abruptly*) I'm going to investigate. . . . (*He commences to walk after* NAARAH.)

POL (*recoiling*): Ohad! Where are you off to? (*He takes no notice of her.*) Kenaz! He couldn't be going after—— ? It isn't possible! (*She runs into the lane.*) Ohad! Ohad! (*He has disappeared from view. She returns slowly to sink on to the seat.*) Well, I'm damned! Do you think he's going to take her back, Kenaz?

KENAZ (*savagely*): What do I know? First Naarah, then Ohad—the whole world's turning upside down, it seems! (POL *begins to cry.*) Yes, and we are left behind, you and I—in the same boat—stranded high and dry! We are, in short, as you so wittily expressed it, among the damned, my cherub!

CURTAIN

NOTICE

As a condition of allowing the public performance of *Ohad's Woman*, the Lord Chamberlain requires the omission of the word "bloody" (on page 59) from the spoken dialogue.

CHOSEN PEOPLE

CHARACTERS

PHILLIS, a Gentile woman
ADA, a Jewess
RACHEL, Ada's mother
BARNABAS ⎫
PETER ⎪
PAUL ⎬ Apostles
MATTHEW ⎭

Scene: Vestibule of the Christian Synagogue in Antioch
Time: Afternoon in the Summer of A.D. 48

Among the various synagogues ministering to the populous city of Antioch, an unpretentious but well-appointed dwelling-house has been converted into the headquarters of the rapidly growing Christian sect. A front room, upon which the curtain rises, combines the uses of a vestibule and an outer office. The street door is on the spectator's left: facing it, a curtained opening gives access to the meeting-hall and other rooms. The furniture is plain: a wooden cupboard and a chest or two against the back wall, a small table on the near-side of the curtained opening, chairs here and there. A branched candelabrum, suspended from the ceiling, gives a clue to the character of the place.

[MATTHEW, *a shrunken, anxious-eyed old man, sits stooping low over the table, writing laboriously on a roll of parchment. He wears a long, shabby black gown, with a loose girdle. As he reaches the end of a sentence, he pauses in a reverie. There is a gentle knock at the street door, presently repeated.*

MATTHEW (*looking up*): Is someone at the door? (*He hastily secretes the roll in a large pocket of his gown, and rises, as* PHILLIS, *a woman in early middle age, travel-stained and shouldering a bundle, staggers through the door, in response to the question.*)

PHILLIS: May I come inside?

MATTHEW: Of course! (*He goes to meet her.*) All visitors are welcome! But first let me assist you. (*He helps her to a chair.*)

PHILLIS: Thanks. (*She lowers her bundle to the ground, and seats herself.*) They told me this was a synagogue.

MATTHEW: So it is.

PHILLIS: Are you the minister?

75

MATTHEW: Bless you, no, I'm not anyone of importance—only old Matthew.

PHILLIS: I'm looking for a job.

MATTHEW: I see.

PHILLIS: I thought they might be wanting a Sabbath-*goy*. (*As he does not answer.*) I'm accustomed to the work. I've managed for Jews nearly all my life, and I'm a good cook and needle-woman.

MATTHEW (*sympathetically*): You've come a long journey, by the look of things. I dare say you're hungry.

PHILLIS: Not particularly.

MATTHEW: Let me get you something from our food store. (*He goes to a cupboard.*)

PHILLIS (*dully*): That's all you can do for me, I suppose.

MATTHEW: Now, did I say that? . . . Wait, I'll bring the table over. . . . You'll feel better after a little refreshment. Then you can tell me all about it! (*By this time, the table, with a loaf, a jug and a cup on it, is laid before her.*) Some bread, eh? (*He takes the loaf and breaks it.*)

PHILLIS (*looking at him in surprise*): You haven't washed your hands!

MATTHEW (*smiling*): I see you know all the rules!

PHILLIS: I ought to! I was married to a Jew once. They made me a proselyte of the gate.

MATTHEW: Then you are really not a *goy* at all!

PHILLIS: That's not what his family thought.

MATTHEW: They were stand-offish?

PHILLIS: Not specially. (*Looking about her.*) This must be a funny synagogue.

MATTHEW: You're not eating anything. Let me pour you out some milk?

PHILLIS: No, thank you. I can't eat like this—by myself. I'm not a beggar!

MATTHEW (*cheerfully*): *I* am. I've been living on charity for years. . . . Won't you eat something if I keep you company?

PHILLIS (*slightly bewildered*): Perhaps I will then.

MATTHEW: Good! (*He puts a piece of bread in his mouth.*)

PHILLIS: Don't you even say the blessing?

MATTHEW: Sometimes. If I happen to feel like it. . . . (*Rising.*) Do you know what I'm feeling like at this moment? Wait! (*He*

76

collects the milk jug.) I'll put the milk away first—and get another cup. . . . (*He returns from the cupboard with a more ornate jug, from which he proceeds to fill both cups.*)

PHILLIS: *Wine ! !*

MATTHEW: Reserved for our honoured guests ! And now, if you please ! (*He lifts his cup.*) " Blessed art thou, O Lord our God, King of the Universe, who createst the fruit of the vine." . . . (*They both drink.*) Do you happen to care for nuts?

PHILLIS: Nuts, did you say ?

MATTHEW: Perhaps you've never tasted any. (*He returns to the cupboard to fetch a plateful.*) I take them instead of meat. Here ! Don't be afraid of them.

PHILLIS (*as she munches*): Do you not eat meat—ever ?

MATTHEW: No. It saves a lot of argument. I never cared much for it, anyway. I'm what they call a vegetarian.

PHILLIS: A vegetarian ! Oh dear ! (*She begins to laugh.*) I'm so sorry ! It's only the wine. . . .

MATTHEW: Of course it is ! . . . " Wine that maketh glad the heart of man !" Another piece of bread ? (*Breaking it for her.*) How do you like the nuts ?

PHILLIS: I think they're nice—I think *you* are, too ! (*She eats and drinks at her ease.*) That's enough ! Now I feel—strong.

MATTHEW: Good ! Let me just put these things out of the way. (*As she half-rises to help.*) You sit quiet now—after your long journey.

PHILLIS (*while he clears up*): I really don't know what you think I'm doing here. . . . Your honoured guest, indeed !

MATTHEW: Well, you see, dear sister (*returning to her, and breaking it gently*), we are unfortunately not able to receive you as a Sabbath-*goy*. (*Her face falls.*) The truth is, we don't employ outside assistance.

PHILLIS: Don't you even observe the Sabbath ?

MATTHEW: Not strictly. Rather, not all of us observe it strictly. It is a matter of individual choice.

PHILLIS: And I thought I knew all there was to be known about Jews !

MATTHEW: You are a stranger in Antioch ?

PHILLIS: I used to live here—many years ago.

MATTHEW: Did you ever hear the word " Christian " ?

PHILLIS: Isn't that what they call bad characters ?

MATTHEW: Yes. That's what they used to call *us*. They didn't like us, you see. But we rather liked their name for us. So now we call *ourselves* Christians. Only we've given it a different meaning.

PHILLIS: What does it mean for you?

MATTHEW: As a Proselyte, you will have heard of our Messiah?

PHILLIS: Yes, I was instructed in the Prophets.

MATTHEW: We Christians believe that the Messiah—the Christ—has already lived among us. And has left us again for a time. He was rejected and put to death, on the cross.

PHILLIS (*in a whisper*): Was it the Nazarene? I have heard about him.

MATTHEW (*his eyes lighting up*): And you want to hear more? I *knew* you would, the moment I set eyes on you!

PHILLIS: So that's why you made such a fuss of me! How typically Jewish!

MATTHEW (*anxiously*): You are not offended?

PHILLIS: Offended! No, I am not offended. (*She suddenly sighs deeply.*) Only I am very tired.

MATTHEW: I can see that.

PHILLIS: Not my body so much. . . . (*Simply.*) If you had sent me away, I was going to drown myself. Perhaps you saw *that*, too?

MATTHEW (*gently*): The Beloved Christ said, " Come unto me all you who labour and are heavy-laden, and I will give you rest."

PHILLIS (*with an effort*): I shall be all right once I get a job.

MATTHEW: You have been searching for long?

PHILLIS (*nodding*): Ever since—since——

MATTHEW: Since your husband died?

PHILLIS: I didn't say he was dead.

MATTHEW (*tactfully*): We must find something useful for you to do in Antioch.

PHILLIS (*mechanically*): That'll be fine.

MATTHEW: But it isn't only a job you're seeking.

PHILLIS: I'm seeking release—from myself.

MATTHEW: I know, sister. And you've come to the right place.

PHILLIS: I've been told that in other places. Oh, I believe in your God, and I try to pray to him. Perhaps if I were one of you, it would be different.

MATTHEW: You haven't heard the good news yet.

PHILLIS: And what is your good news?

MATTHEW (*restraining himself*): *That* you must learn from one of the others.

PHILLIS (*curiously*): Why can't *you* tell me?

MATTHEW: Because I'm not worthy—I should tell you all wrong. (*With a burst.*) I'm only a blundering old idiot. . . . (*Solemnly.*) Saul himself shall impart the good news to you.

PHILLIS: Saul? Is he your chief ruler?

MATTHEW (*shaking his head*): We don't have rulers here—only prophets and teachers—with their different gifts.

PHILLIS: Then is Saul the one in authority?

MATTHEW: No. I don't think it would be correct to say that. There are others with authority as well. . . . Peter, who was our leader in Jerusalem in the early days—we all look up to him; but he doesn't really live in Antioch, though he often stays here. But then Saul travels a lot too—and he's a much younger man. And, besides, there's James, who certainly has authority in Jerusalem. . . . It's all rather difficult to explain. But Saul's different from all of them. He's so tremendous! I sometimes think he must be the greatest man in the world! (*He pauses.*)

PHILLIS: Tell me more about him.

MATTHEW: Well, would you believe it, he used to be our greatest enemy—and such a ferocious one! He broke up our community in Jerusalem—we were all terrified of him!—and some of the brethren fled here for safety, and that was how this synagogue of ours came into existence. Then suddenly the truth was revealed to him, and he came over to our side. And now—I can't tell you all the hardships he's endured—imprisonments, floggings, every kind of indignity—all for the sake of spreading our message in new regions. . . . You never saw such energy! And you never heard such preaching! Perhaps we are all a little scared of him still—but really I don't see how anyone can help admiring the man. . . . I'm not tiring you, am I?

PHILLIS: You're doing me good! It's always like this when I get among Jews again. I feel somehow at home with your ways and feelings. I could never have married anyone but a Jew. Queer, isn't it? There's something I like about all Jews—even bad ones.

MATTHEW: Queer—and generous. Because your husband was a bad one.

PHILLIS: I never said so.

MATTHEW: He divorced you.

PHILLIS: He had a right to.

MATTHEW: According to the law of Moses, perhaps. The Beloved used to say that our divorce laws were made for hardhearted people, and that a man who, for any reason whatever, sent a faithful wife out of his house was much to be condemned.

PHILLIS: A faithful wife, you say. He would not have condemned my husband, then. (MATTHEW *is taken aback.*) Why did I have to let that out, now?

MATTHEW: It was my fault—my usual pig-headedness! I am so sorry.

PHILLIS: Yes, we were getting on famously, weren't we? (*She rises.*) Thank you for all your hospitality.

MATTHEW (*aghast*): You're not going away? Oh no, *no*, you mustn't!

PHILLIS: You can't want to be associated with a woman like me.

MATTHEW: Don't say such things! Oh, please, please.

PHILLIS: Tell me one thing: is this or isn't this a respectable synagogue?

MATTHEW: You ask me such difficult questions! It all depends what you mean by respectable. Do you consider me a respectable person? Shall I tell you what I used to do for my living?

PHILLIS: You weren't brought up to be a good Jew: that's evident.

MATTHEW: I was brought up to prey on my fellow men: I was that most shameful and odious of criminals, a Publican. There! . . . Yet the Beloved himself chose to be associated with me, and when they sneered at him for keeping bad company, he answered: "It is the sick that have need of a physician, not the sound."

PHILLIS (*arrested*): That was a true word.

MATTHEW (*anxiously*): Only wait—wait! Promise me you will!

PHILLIS: And see your physician, Saul? Does it mean so much to you?

[*At that moment there enters from the inner room* BARNABAS, *a man considerably younger than* MATTHEW, *stalwart and dignified in bearing, a model of quiet zeal and efficiency, at present over-worked and preoccupied.*

BARNABAS: Matthew——

MATTHEW (*turning with a start*): Ah! It is one of the others— Brother Joseph. We call him Barnabas: that means, son of encouragement. . . .

BARNABAS (*to* PHILLIS): Pardon me. (*He turns to* MATTHEW.) Have you found that list of subscriptions ?

MATTHEW: The list ? Oh, that memory of mine ! Did you want it particularly at this moment, brother ?

PHILLIS (*edging towards the door, to* MATTHEW): I will return later, perhaps . . .

MATTHEW (*quickly*): No, you don't ! (*He darts across to bar her way.*) We mustn't let her go, brother ! She is a seeker—in urgent need— already interested.

BARNABAS: Have you taken her name and address ?

MATTHEW (*to* PHILLIS): Did I ask you ?

PHILLIS: My name is Phillis.

MATTHEW: Phillis. I will write it down at once. (*He goes to the table to inscribe it on a tablet.*)

PHILLIS (*as he writes*): It's a stupid name. . . . I have no address.

MATTHEW: Our sister is a stranger to Antioch.

BARNABAS (*to* PHILLIS): We have a meeting for inquirers to-morrow afternoon at six. I hope you will be able to come.

PHILLIS: Thank you.

MATTHEW: You are not to go yet ! (*To* BARNABAS.) I wanted her to meet Saul, brother.

BARNABAS (*in gentle reproof*): Our brother Paul is unfortun-ately——

MATTHEW: Did I call him Saul again ? I'm incorrigible !

BARNABAS (*kindly*): Don't distress yourself, brother. The name is not important. But time—every moment, where Paul is con-cerned—*that* is of importance !

MATTHEW: I know. I should have remembered. . . . I was thinking only of our sister's welfare. . . . If I weren't so useless ! Would *you* perhaps speak a few words to her ?

BARNABAS: Brother, brother ! My school syllabus !

MATTHEW (*growing more agitated in his confusion*): Of course ! And all your administrative duties ! That list of subscriptions. Where did I put it, now ? (*To* PHILLIS.) Our congregation is growing so rapidly, you see. Only think, we had two sets of twins last month ! (*To* BARNABAS.) Simeon called here about his father's funeral. He will notify all the mourners for us. Won't that be a help ! (*There is a knock at the door.*) There's another of them, I expect !

BARNABAS: I'll have to manage without the list, that's all.

MATTHEW (*to* PHILLIS): It seems we are compelled to undertake these worldly offices. Isn't it awful!

BARNABAS: Will you see who is at the door?

MATTHEW (*keeping his eye on* PHILLIS): Yes, if you'll sit down first —over here, please! (*Practically forcing her into a chair, he hurries to the front door, but before he can reach it, it has opened to admit a good-looking and well-dressed young Jewess.*) It is Nathan's daughter. (*Addressing her.*) Come in, Ada.

ADA (*shortly*): I want to speak to Paul, please.

BARNABAS (*advancing*): Is there anything I can do for you?

ADA (*bitingly*): Yes. You can tell Paul I want to see him—at once.

BARNABAS: That is not possible.

ADA: Hasn't he returned yet?

BARNABAS: Our brother is at prayer. He returned hardly an hour ago.

ADA: Very well, I'll wait.

BARNABAS: I fear he will not have time to see anyone to-day.

ADA: I'll wait, just the same. (*A pause.*) There was talk of Peter coming back.

BARNABAS: We are expecting him before the Sabbath. . . . If you would like to have a word with me in private. . . .

ADA (*as* PHILLIS *rises*): Please don't move on my account. (*To* BARNABAS.) I am sure you must have many duties to attend to.

BARNABAS (*with a touch of asperity*): My duties include the final arrangements for a ceremony of marriage.

ADA: Then you can cancel them!

BARNABAS: What! But I had a talk with your father only this morning.

ADA: I know you did. (*Compressing her lips.*) That's what I've come to see Paul about.

BARNABAS: If you have any complaint to make——

ADA: I prefer to make it to Paul in person. (*Observing* MATTHEW's *woebegone expression.*) I am sorry to have interrupted everyone.

MATTHEW (*seizing his opportunity*): If you are waiting, may I present our sister Phillis—a newcomer to our congregation.

[BARNABAS, *in perplexity, retires to the back of the stage, and begins to search in the chests for the missing list of subscriptions.*]

ADA: Greeting, sister. (*A pause.*) You are attracted to the teachings?

82

PHILLIS: I know very little . . .

MATTHEW: Phillis has only just arrived here.

ADA: Where from, if I may ask?

PHILLIS: My home is near Sidon in Phœnicia.

ADA (*warming up*): That's interesting. Alex—my future husband—is a Phœnician. His people used to be followers of Zeno, the Stoic, who came from the same country, as you probably know. Zeno's philosophy is satisfying up to a point, of course, but it leads you to despair of everything in the end, doesn't it? Alex's childhood was made miserable by the feeling that life had nothing to offer except an endless battling between good and evil. He says that the revelation of a loving God came to him just as the use of his limbs might come to a paralytic.

PHILLIS: Yes, yes.

ADA: And then with the further revelation, through Paul——You haven't heard Paul yet, I suppose?

PHILLIS: No. The further revelation, you say?

ADA: I mean the assurance that by the sacrifice of our Messiah on the Cross the Kingdom promised to the seed of Abraham is thrown open to all mankind. In the old days, only Jews could hope to be admitted. Now that barrier has been broken down.

[*A grim-faced matron has entered unobtrusively from the street, and stands listening in the doorway.*

Salvation is granted freely to every human being willing to be baptized in the faith.

RACHEL (*the newcomer*): And who is obedient to the Law!

ADA (*the least surprised of the company*): Mother! I might have guessed! So you followed me here to make a scene——

BARNABAS (*coming forward, cordially*): Will you not come forward, Rachel?

RACHEL (*advancing*): Her father thought I ought to warn you. (ADA *gives a short laugh.*) What has she been saying?

BARNABAS (*turning to* MATTHEW): Sister Phillis would perhaps like to see our collection of sacred books.

MATTHEW (*with alacrity*): I am sure she would! (*Beckoning to* PHILLIS.) Please to accompany me. . . . Through here. (*He leads her through the curtained partition.*)

BARNABAS: Now! (*After waiting, vainly, for a lead.*) Am I to understand that the marriage is not to take place?

RACHEL (*noncommittal*): If she so chooses.

ADA (*mockingly*): In fact, nothing would give you greater satisfaction !

RACHEL: I didn't say that.

ADA: But it's true, isn't it ? You've been against my marrying Alex, both of you, from the first. (*As* RACHEL *would protest.*) Oh, I know you withdrew your formal objection when Alex became a Jew. Only because James had to sanction the engagement.

RACHEL: Rabbi Jacob—(*correcting herself*) James—advised us that no breach of the Torah was in question. That was good enough.

ADA: Good enough ! But a disappointment to your hopes, all the same.

RACHEL: We should naturally have preferred a son-in-law whose family was known to us.

ADA: A son-in-law of Jewish blood, you mean. Why not speak plainly ?

RACHEL: Very well. As your mother, I would have preferred it. Because I think Jewish men make better husbands than——

ADA: Than *goys*—heathens, eh ? Heathens—that's all they are to you: Alex, with his rich, generous nature, and his father and mother, such a wonderfully unselfish couple. . . . Heathens ! Only to be tolerated so long as they defer to us, model their lives on our superior ways ! And you call yourself a follower of the Lord Jesus ! Well, you can say what you like—I happen to think my future husband's family every bit as good as my own.

RACHEL: An infatuated chit would be the best judge, of course !

BARNABAS: But—one moment, please ! (*To* ADA.) Your future husband, you call him ? I thought you said you wanted me to cancel the arrangements for your marriage ?

ADA (*looking away*): I'd rather my marriage were arranged by someone not holding my parents' ideas.

RACHEL: So that's it ! This synagogue isn't good enough for her !

ADA: That isn't what I said !

RACHEL: And if the Rabbi takes you at your word—and decides to have nothing more to do with you ! What, then ? Will you find another synagogue ?

ADA: I'd rather not discuss the matter with you. I won't discuss it with *anyone*—till I've heard what Paul has to say.

RACHEL (*to* BARNABAS): Where is Rabbi Paul ?

BARNABAS: I have already explained to your daughter that he is not to be seen.

ADA: And I have told him that I am going to wait till I see him, whether he likes it or not. So you might just as well go home.

RACHEL (*grimly folding her arms*): If you are going to wait, so am I ! (*She takes a chair facing her.*)

[*A short pause. Then* MATTHEW's *head appears through the curtain.*

MATTHEW: Barnabas ! I've found that list ! . . . Might we come back now ?

ADA: Oh, please do ! We should so welcome your company.

MATTHEW (*advancing with* PHILLIS *at his rear*): Only think—I must have left it when I was dusting yesterday. (*He delivers a roll of parchment to* BARNABAS.)

BARNABAS: Thank you. (*In a murmur, to the others.*) I will see if it is possible to approach Paul. . . . He will be much displeased.

[*With a heavy sigh and a troubled face, he goes quickly out.*

PHILLIS (*embarrassed*): I really oughtn't to stay here any longer.

ADA: We must be making a bad impression on you.

PHILLIS: I didn't mean it like that. . . .

MATTHEW (*artfully*): In that case, you must sit down and make yourself at home ! (*He draws up another chair for her.*) You won't find it difficult, I know. (*To the others.*) Our sister was telling me that she is always at her ease among our people.

RACHEL (*politely*): Perhaps she is of Hebrew extraction.

PHILLIS: No, I don't think that is the reason. (*She seats herself.*) I think it is because of something that happened to me when I was a child.

ADA (*after a pause.*) Won't you tell us, please.

PHILLIS: If you would like me to. I heard of it from my mother many years afterwards. (*Again she pauses.*) We were living in a small village near the sea. I was taken ill there. Father had just died, and it was a distressing illness. Mother tried one remedy after another. She was a very determined woman, and I was her only child. (*Another pause.*) One day she heard some talk about a strange man who had come to stay in a neighbouring village. No one knew much about him, but Mother said she felt all at once that he was the only man in the world who could make me well again. It was a kind of vision, something unaccountable. So she sought out this man, but it wasn't easy to speak to him, because of a bodyguard of friends who hurried him away whenever she came near. Mother learnt afterwards that the man had come into our country to rest after a long spell of work among his own people. He was a Jew, a holy man, and a healer.

MATTHEW (*in a low voice*): Did she say how he looked?

PHILLIS: She said she could hardly bear to importune him, he looked so tired and so sad. Only her love for me was too strong, and in the end, she forced her way through to him, fell on her knees, and declared she wouldn't leave until he had heard her petition. His first words nearly froze her.

ADA (*after a pause*): What did he say?

PHILLIS: He said, " I am not sent but unto the lost sheep of Israel."

RACHEL: He may not have meant it unkindly.

PHILLIS: He spoke out of a good heart, Mother used to say. Hers was a good heart too, so perhaps that made a bond between them. When she told him what she had come for, he sighed and asked if she thought it right that bread provided for the children of the house should be given to the dogs; but she saw that he was smiling at her.

MATTHEW (*softly, as before*): Did she tell you how she answered his question?

PHILLIS: She answered that even the dogs lick up the crumbs that fall from the children's table.

ADA: That was lovely!

PHILLIS: Yes. And he loved her for it. She could feel his love travelling right through her—that was how she described it. She knew almost before he spoke that all her worrying was at an end. His love, even from that distance, had expelled the disease out of my body. Can you understand that?

MATTHEW: Yes. All of us can.

PHILLIS: Mother told me the story just before she died. Often I have had a mad idea of trying to find the man. . . . I think the reason I like being with Jews is that they remind me of the love I owe to him.

[*In the hush that follows,* PETER *enters silently from the street—a commanding figure, with grizzled curly hair and a weatherbeaten face, leaning heavily on his staff. At the same moment,* BARNABAS *reappears from the opposite side of the room.*

BARNABAS (*recoiling*): *Peter!* (*Advancing with outstretched arms.*) A welcome surprise!

PETER: Well, Joe. (*Embraces him.*) Peace and grace upon all of you.

MATTHEW (*excitedly*): Simon bar Jonas, you come opportunely.

PETER (*grasping his hand*): How are you, old friend?

86

BARNABAS: We weren't expecting you before Sabbath eve.

PETER: I had to rearrange my plans.

MATTHEW: You remember that woman in Syro-Phœnicia?

PETER (*only half-listening*): Let me sit down. It has been a tiring journey. (BARNABAS *helps him to a chair. Seeing* RACHEL.) I know your face.

BARNABAS: Rachel, wife of Nathan, the goldsmith. (*Aside.*) Some water, Matthew.

PETER: From Jerusalem, of course. How is your husband?

RACHEL: Not well, I am sorry to say.

PETER (*as* MATTHEW *brings him a cup of water*): Oh, thank you. (*He drinks.*)

ADA (*standing before him with sudden determination*): Excuse me, sir. I am Nathan's daughter. I want to ask an important question.

PETER (*putting the cup down*): Well, my dear?

[MATTHEW, *thwarted in his attempts to capture* PETER's *attention, retires to the back of the stage, where* PHILLIS *gravitates to his side.*

ADA: I have heard it said that when you were living in Joppa, you once made a special journey to Cæsarea to visit a Roman officer, and dined with him in his house.

RACHEL (*with sarcasm*): She must believe everything she hears, naturally.

ADA (*to* PETER): Is the story true?

PETER (*slowly*): Perfectly true. Cornelius was one of the most generous patrons of the synagogue at Cæsarea.

ADA: And I have heard how, later, when he knelt down before you, you made him rise, saying, " I am only a man like you."

PETER (*almost inaudibly*): Yes, I said that.

ADA: Is it also true that you have lately agreed to have no more meals in Gentile houses?

[PETER *stares before him without answering.*

RACHEL: Impertinence! What business is it of yours?

ADA: That is easily answered. (*To* PETER.) They are quoting your example, sir, in commanding me to insult the family of my betrothed.

PETER (*weary but patiently*): Who are doing this? May I hear all the facts of the case?

RACHEL: There is no question of her insulting anybody, Rabbi.

ADA: I say it is insulting to refuse to accept hospitality.

RACHEL: It all depends on the circumstances. If they were sensible people, they would offer their hospitality in a form that would be acceptable.

ADA: You mean, go to the endless trouble and expense of scrapping all their pots and pans, turning their whole household upside down.

RACHEL: For sincere converts, it would not be a trouble.

ADA: Sincere converts to what? They are sincere followers of our Lord.

RACHEL: And wasn't our Lord an upholder of the Law? Did he not declare that until Heaven and earth should pass away, not the smallest jot or tittle of the Law was to be altered?

ADA: It is not what goes into the mouth, but what comes out of it that makes a man unclean. . . . Haven't you quoted those as his very words, Matthew? (*She looks round to fix him.*)

MATTHEW (*miserably*): Oh please, please—don't ask me to take sides.

RACHEL: It isn't a question of what is clean or unclean—it is a question of obeying the Law.

ADA: Surely we left all that behind us in Jerusalem.

RACHEL: Left the Holy Torah behind us? Are you mad as well as ignorant? The Holy Torah which is implanted in the hearts of all who call themselves Jews!

ADA: I call myself a Christian.

RACHEL: And isn't that the same thing, you perverse creature? Do you think we are the less Jews for entering the service of our Anointed One? When our leader, his own brother, directs us to remain faithful.

ADA: Paul is my leader, not James.

RACHEL: Rabbi Paul takes his orders from Jerusalem.

ADA: So you say. (*She looks pointedly at* PETER.)

PETER (*grimly*): Well? I am still waiting to hear the facts.

RACHEL: The facts are perfectly simple, Rabbi Simon. The girl has been disobeying her parents by eating in an un-*kosher* household. Her father sent to Rabbi Jacob for a ruling on the question, and that ruling has now been received from Jerusalem. She has heard it explained in the clearest possible language.

ADA: Yes. I have heard that I am forbidden to have meals with my betrothed in his own Christian home. (*With a gesture to* PETER.) And that I have you and Barnabas to thank for it!

PETER (*turning to* BARNABAS): What does she mean by that, brother?

BARNABAS: For my part, I have done no more than carry out orders. I was careful to refrain from expressing my own opinion. I was not asked for it.

ADA: And were you asked to express Peter's opinion? *Ordered* to express it, I should say? (*As he hesitates.*) Well, sir?

BARNABAS: I was ordered to mention particularly that Peter concurred in the ruling.

PETER (*puzzled*): Let me understand this correctly. Nathan applies for a ruling from James in Jerusalem, and you, Barnabas, communicate that ruling to Nathan. You were ordered, you say, to do so?

BARNABAS: It was included in a special letter of instructions delivered to me personally by Ezra and Symeon.

ADA: Father's closest confederates! I said it was all a put-up job!

RACHEL: How dare you speak like that!

BARNABAS (*to* PETER): Could we not confer privately?

PETER: Yes, that will be best. (*Abruptly.*) No, brother, it would be sheer cowardice on my part! At least I can come into the open. (*After a short pause.*) That my name should have been brought into this controversy by James has, I must own, disagreeably surprised me. I never authorized it.

BARNABAS: It was certainly a disagreeable surprise to me, brother.

PETER: I will make a clean breast of what has passed between us. For several weeks, I have been in treaty with James in consequence of complaints about my laxity in these food matters.

BARNABAS: But surely all that was hammered out in our talks last year?

PETER: It seems that James has never been happy—or, for that matter, really clear—about the outcome of the discussion. And very great pressure has been brought to bear on him. You know what the feeling is in Jerusalem. I have been torn both ways, brother. We are a sacred fellowship, and must hold together at all costs. That makes necessary a central authority. Rivalry between communities each bearing the name of Christ is unthinkable. It is equally unthinkable that we should cut ourselves adrift from the Lord's own kith and kin in our Holy City. James appealed to me on all these grounds.

BARNABAS: To go back on our understanding?

PETER: On a misunderstanding, according to him. And we are speaking, remember, of James the Just. (*With bowed head.*) Moreover, far be it from me to reproach a man for going back on his word. . . . (*After a pause.*) Still, I never authorized him to use my name. I merely agreed, after much persuasion, as a matter of expediency, and so that my example at least should not be a hindrance, that I would endeavour to persuade my own Christian converts to conform to the food laws.

[*An uncomfortable silence.*

ADA: And have you any hope of succeeding ? (*More hotly.*) And do you think it either right or reasonable ?

PETER: What I think personally is quite another matter, sister. Between ourselves——

RACHEL: Before you say any more, I think you ought to know that there is a stranger present.

MATTHEW (*protesting*): Surely not a stranger, sister. (*To* PETER.) Phillis here is——

PHILLIS (*coming forward*): Of course I am a stranger ! And, for that reason (*turning to* PETER), before you say any more, Master (*appealing to all*), I ask leave as a privilege, to make a humble proposal.

PETER (*patiently*): By all means.

PHILLIS: I know very well what Miss Ada meant when she spoke just now of the trouble of turning an ordinary Phœnician household into a " clean " one. I would be glad and grateful of an opportunity of saving someone that trouble. I've lived and worked among strict Jewish people most of my life, and I dare say I know as much about your ritual laws as anyone here present. (*Turning to* ADA.) If you'll pardon my asking, what sort of staff does your intended's mother employ ?

ADA: Only an old cook and two boys.

PHILLIS: I could manage them easily enough. If she'll say the word, I'll come in and arrange things so that the family will hardly notice any inconvenience. And I'll guarantee to keep on the right side of everybody concerned ! (ADA *is too bewildered to know what to say.*) Won't you think it over—for my sake ? I'm only asking for a chance to make myself useful.

ADA (*shaken*): It's extraordinarily good of you.

PHILLIS (*earnestly*): Listen to me, Miss Ada. I know what I'm talking about. Don't fall out with your own people, if there's any way of avoiding it. It won't make your married life any easier believe me.

ADA: I—I shall have to see what Alex thinks. I—I—— (*She suddenly bursts into tears.*)

RACHEL (*visibly relieved*): That's better. (*To* PETER.) She'll be all right after a good cry. She's not a bad girl at heart. (*To* PHILLIS.) I think that's an admirable suggestion of yours. I'm sure we are all very much indebted to you. (*Turning to* BARNABAS.) May we leave it to you to arrange the details? (*Without waiting for an answer, she goes over to* ADA.) Come, Ada. It's time we returned to your father. He'll be growing anxious about us.

[*As* ADA *rises unsteadily, a harsh voice is heard through the partition, calling for* BARNABAS. *There is an instantaneous shift of tension.*

MATTHEW (*to* PHILLIS): That's Saul's voice—Paul's——

[*And* PAUL *bursts upon the scene, a shortish man, going bald, bandy-legged, with eyebrows nearly joining, and a hook nose, and withal, mysteriously, "full of grace." He brandishes a sheet of parchment.*

PAUL: Barnabas! Here, what do you make of this? (*Seeing* PETER, *and stammering in his excitement.*) P-P-P-Peter! You're the man I want! Would you believe it, James has been got at again by those damned circumcisionist busy-bodies! Now we shall have to fight the whole m-m-maddening business out with him again! When was this drivelling document delivered here, Barnabas?

BARNABAS: Ezra and Symeon Niger arrived with it yesterday. They brought a verbal message as well.

PAUL: Ezra and Symeon! Those snakes! I might have guessed . . . Ezra, Symeon and Nathan, eh? (*He taps the paper.*) The voice is the voice of James, but we know where the smell comes from!

BARNABAS: Nathan's wife is present.

PAUL: So I see. And these Phœnician converts all the fuss is about? I can't read their names: The writing's nearly as bad as my own!

ADA (*coming forward*): They are the parents of Alexander, the man I am going to marry.

PAUL: You? Oh, you're Nathan's daughter, eh? I remember now. So there's been a regular upset at home, it seems.

BARNABAS (*hastily intervening*): I called on Nathan this morning, as directed.

PAUL: What, already? I think you might have waited to consult me. You knew I'd be back to-day.

BARNABAS: Ezra and Symeon insisted that James had made a special point of the urgency.

PAUL (*drily*): I see. Well! (*Turning to* RACHEL.) You can tell Nathan from me that this ruling is all wrong, and will be rectified at the earliest possible moment.

RACHEL (*nervously*): Oh, but there's no need now. Everything's been settled.

PAUL (*sharply*): Settled? On what terms?

RACHEL: That hardly concerns the outside world. It was all a family quarrel.

PAUL: N-n-nonsense, woman! It was—and is—a quarrel as to whether persons baptized in this synagogue are required, for any purposes whatever, to observe the ritual laws of our Palestinian forefathers. And I say they are not—they are free of the Law, once and for ever. (*Glaring about him.*) Is that quite clear to everybody?

ADA (*ecstatically*): To me it is crystal-clear, glory be to God! Once and for ever!

RACHEL (*turning from* BARNABAS *to* PETER): Are neither of you going to speak?

PETER (*clasping his hands*): Lord, give me strength. (*He faces* PAUL.) Brother, I speak under constraint. I cannot acquiesce . . .

PAUL (*staring at him*): Peter!

PETER: You may say it is none of my business: it is true, as we have agreed, that your charge is to the Gentiles, as mine, nearer home, to Jewry. I plead for the good of all. Think how our enemies will rejoice to learn that an edict received from the fount-head of our authority is to be disregarded—nay, flouted!

PAUL: What other course is open to us? Are we to surrender to crazy bigots who would make nonsense of all my preaching?

PETER: I say we should proceed with circumspection, sacrificing, if necessary, the immediate to the ultimate objective.

PAUL (*impatiently*): Tell me this, Peter: Are you prepared to sacrifice your own freedom?

PETER: What do you mean by that? I have told James that I will use my influence to bring my own Gentile friends into line.

PAUL: Have you told him that you propose in future to put on your phylacteries morning and evening, recite the correct blessings on every occasion, keep the Sabbath and all the festivals punctiliously—and incidentally see that your wife prepares your own meals in strict accordance with the thousand and one niceties of the Law ? (PETER *is silent.*) You do not answer. You live like a Gentile yourself, yet you propose to ask Gentiles to live like Jews ! Pshaw !

[PETER *is badly shaken.*

RACHEL (*boldly*) : May I say a word, please ? No one could accuse me and my husband of living like Gentiles. Since childhood we have held faithfully to the letter of the Law.

PAUL (*rounding on her*) : And you would compel every member of this congregation to do likewise ?

RACHEL : I would. If they want our privileges, they must be willing to pay the price.

PAUL : And your husband shares that opinion ?

RACHEL : He certainly does.

PAUL (*violently*) : Then this synagogue is no place for either of you ! You are accursed, the pair of you—accursed, do you hear me ? I expel you from the Lord's table !

RACHEL (*blenching*) : You can't do that ! We have nowhere else to go. We were among the first believers in Antioch, baptized twice over.

PAUL : The true faith is not in you. Christ crucified is not in you.

RACHEL (*hotly*) : Who are you to tell us these things ? Once you were openly our persecutor ; now you claim the right to rule our lives, and are leading us into apostasy. (*Turning to the others.*) Why should we submit to the tyrant ?

PAUL (*controlling himself*) : Answer her, B-B-Barnabas.

BARNABAS : Because you were appointed by the Risen Lord.

RACHEL : So he says ! Where are his witnesses ? You have only his mouthings for it ! Others have spoken with tongues as well.

BARNABAS : Be silent, woman !

RACHEL : Is that your justice ? This upstart may order me into the outer darkness, and I must be silent ! Simon bar Jonas (*turning to* PETER), you on whom the Blessed Lord founded our Christian order—I appeal against a heretic's judgment.

PETER (*brokenly*) : I am sorry, but what can I say except that his reproof of me was only too well deserved. . . . (*To* PAUL.) Yes, I'm an old weathercock, as usual, brother. But, stay, I cannot allow you to pronounce curses. (*To* RACHEL.) The curse I lift from you.

PAUL : She's not saved. What's the difference ? (*With a shrug.*) I never can keep my temper, anyway.

PETER: You can keep the vision, though ! No barriers between the nations ! I'll try to stand by that in future. And you, Barnabas ?

BARNABAS: I'll stand by Paul in future.

PETER: If you don't like it, Rachel, I'm sorry, but you will have to go.

RACHEL (*pursing her lips*): We'll see about that !

ADA (*timidly to* BARNABAS): My marriage—if you please——— (*He smiles at her.*) Before the new moon ? (*He nods.*)

PAUL (*briskly*): What's next on the agenda ? (*He moves towards the exit.*)

MATTHEW (*intervening*): Brother S—Paul ! I have a favour to ask. (*He turns, with a gesture to* PHILLIS, *who slowly shakes her head.*) Another time, perhaps . . . (*He draws back again.*)

PAUL (*to* PETER *and* BARNABAS): We'll adjourn to my room. (*Sincerely.*) Peace be with you all.

[*Amid a subdued " Amen " he passes through the curtains, followed by* PETER *and* BARNABAS.

RACHEL (*defiantly*): Let them go ! (*Turning to* ADA.) Your father will know how to deal with all this ! We'll call a protest meeting at once. And only wait till Rabbi Jacob hears of it !

ADA: Wait ? But I'm keeping Alex waiting ! I must fly ! (*As she turns to go.*) Don't expect me for supper, Mother.

RACHEL: What ! (*Fearfully.*) So you are going again to that house ? (ADA *smiles pityingly.*) You owe obedience to your father still !

ADA: Paul is my Father. (RACHEL *recoils as if struck. To* PHILLIS.) You'll come and see us after we're married, I hope. . . . (*Moving to the door.*) Grace, everybody !

RACHEL: Come back. (*As* ADA *disappears.*) Ada ! *Ada !* (*The door is closed. She tosses her head.*) Silly girl ! She'll come to her senses presently ! (*She sways slightly, then starts, seeing* MATTHEW *and* PHILLIS *converge towards her.*) I mustn't stay here. I've been expelled, haven't I ? (*She breaks down, on her way to the door, and vainly mustering the remnants of her dignity, stumbles out before they can prevent it.*)

PHILLIS: Poor old thing ! Will they take her back, do you think ?

MATTHEW (*with a sigh*): Not if Paul has his way. . . . And her ideas are all wrong, you know.

94

PHILLIS (*warmly*): She can't help her ideas. And she's a good-hearted creature—anyone can see that. They ought to make allowances. It'll be hard for her not having a synagogue.

MATTHEW: You're disappointed, aren't you? (*She nods.*) There's something I wanted to tell you—about that Healer——

PHILLIS: You needn't tell me. . . . I guessed. (*After a pause.*) It makes no difference. I want to go out and look for him again.

MATTHEW (*a catch in his voice*): Couldn't you—give us a trial?

PHILLIS: It wouldn't be any use. I think Paul's wonderful—only it's a pity his love isn't for everybody.

MATTHEW: The truth is, I don't always understand what he means. Why shouldn't I confess it? It's because I'm no good, you see.

PHILLIS: You'd better come away with me.

MATTHEW (*with a start*): You don't mean that seriously?

PHILLIS: I do. If Ada can have Paul for a father, I would like to adopt you as mine.

MATTHEW (*beside himself*): Me? . . . You really think I might help you along the way? Oh, if I *could!* . . . Only I mustn't be too hopeful. So often I've had nibbles—and each time, before I could land my catch, the fish has slipped away. It's my clumsiness!

PHILLIS: You think of me as a fish to be caught?

MATTHEW: It's how we were trained. Simon—that's Peter—and his brother, Andrew, were fishermen, you see—and the call came to them: " Follow me, and I will make you fishers of men." And so it happened—with some of us. Only I—I've been such a failure! . . . (*Hopefully.*) When would you like to start?

PHILLIS: As soon as you get your belongings together.

MATTHEW: My belongings? Luckily, I haven't anything—except—(*he pauses*) something that I don't like to leave behind, but—(*firmly*) I must. Because it wasn't meant for me to keep.

PHILLIS: What is it?

MATTHEW: Only a few scraps of parchment scrawled over. (*He extracts them from his pocket as he speaks.*) Notes jotted down at odd moments—as many as I could remember of the Beloved's own words. . . . The brethren are expecting him to return to us very soon, but I thought, just in case his coming might be delayed. . . . It's only a notion of mine.

PHILLIS: May I look at the parchment?

MATTHEW (*showing her*): The words are in Hebrew.

PHILLIS: Have you put your name to it?

MATTHEW: No. Why should I do that?

PHILLIS: In time to come, the words might be questioned. . . . Your name would be a testimony. Write it now—clearly!

MATTHEW (*with misgivings*): What if the words should come to be copied and altered and mixed with other men's words—and my name given to other men's mistakes! . . . Oh well, the owner of the name will have been long forgotten. What does it matter? (*He writes.*) And now—where are we to leave you? (*Crossing to the chest.*) Here, I think. (*He kneels down and deposits the manuscript carefully.*) Sleep well, my child! And if it shall please God in his mercy one day to call you forth—no, no, how dare I think it possible! (*He sighs, then rises.*) Now I'm free! Now I can come with you wherever the wind may blow us!

[*She shoulders her bundle, and leads him out into the city of Antioch.*

CURTAIN

NOTE

" But when Peter came to Antioch, I opposed him to his face, because his own conduct condemned him. I said to him, before them all, ' If you, though a Jew, live like a Gentile, how can you compel the Gentiles to live like Jews? ' " So Paul, at a later crisis, in his famous Letter to the Galatians, recalled a scene which learned men have been inquisitive to reconstruct ever since. I have taken the extreme liberty of weaving it into a play " featuring " a third Apostle, Matthew, on the strength of a theory developed by the late Canon Streeter (in his grand work, *The Four Gospels*) that the Gospel called Matthew, in the form known to us, could only have been written in Antioch. To suppose that the Apostle had any hand in that Gospel is, I am aware, unfashionable among present-day commentators, but I do not find their arguments as convincing as the tradition (first recorded by Papias before A.D. 150 and unquestioned for fifteen centuries) that Matthew himself collected the sayings of Jesus subsequently incorporated in " his " Gospel. If Matthew existed at all (which needless to say, is denied by many of the " specialists "), he was undoubtedly a model of self-effacement, and the actual words of Papias—" Matthew compiled the oracles in the Hebrew tongue, but every man translated them as he was able "—seem to typify the irony of his fate. The New Testament is silent as to his life subsequent to the arrest of Jesus, and there is no authority for my " haggadic " interpretation of the kind of man he may have been.

POSTSCRIPT:

Mr. Hugh J. Schonfield, whose scholarly *According to the Hebrews* I am reading as this book goes to press, assures me that the " oracles " referred to by Papias would have consisted only of passages in the Old Testament identifying Jesus as the expected Messiah. He may be right.

FIRST CORINTHIANS

CHARACTERS

JUDITH, wife of Stephanas
SOPHIA, her sister
CHLOE, a widow
MELISSA, her daughter
EULALIA, a feminist
LOIS, a married lady
PHILIP, Judith's son
SOSILAS, Chloe's brother
GLAUCON }
ARTEMAS } litigants
MANES, a slave
TITUS, Paul's emissary

A few slaves (non-speaking) of both sexes

Scene : In the House of Stephanas, Corinth.
Time : A.D. 57

All the female characters, except EULALIA, keep their heads covered, Ionian fashion, throughout the play. Those entering from the street arrive with their faces veiled, removing their veils immediately on crossing the threshold.

_____

A room furnished with a number of chairs, converging about a door in the centre of the back wall, leading into a further room, but leaving a clear passage to a second door, to the fore of the left wall, opening from the street.

[The stage is untenanted at the rise of the curtain. Presently there is a timid knocking at the street door. JUDITH, a middle-aged woman, enters from the inner chamber and, crossing to the other door, opens it, then starts back.

JUDITH : It's Sophie. (*Eagerly.*) Won't you come in ?

[A somewhat older woman enters, uncertain of her reception.

SOPHIA : Judy ! (*They embrace.*) I didn't know whether you'd want to see me.

JUDITH : What, my own sister ! After all these years ! . . . Sit down, dear.

SOPHIA (*obeying*): Yes, we're still sisters, aren't we? And we don't get any younger. That's why I suddenly felt I'd like to call on you . . . while Judah's away on business.

JUDITH: You're well, I hope?

SOPHIA: Thank God. And you? (*She looks at her.*) We've both changed, I suppose.

JUDITH: I hope I have.

SOPHIA: And Stephanas—he's keeping well?

JUDITH: Fairly well. He's away, too—at Ephesus.

SOPHIA: Also on business?

JUDITH (*with some reticence*): On church business.

SOPHIA: He's as keen as ever, then?

JUDITH: We both are. Does that surprise you?

SOPHIA: I only wondered. I suppose (*looking about her*) this is one of your meeting places?

JUDITH: We have meetings here sometimes. . . . Your husband is as bitter as ever?

SOPHIA: Judah's very orthodox.

JUDITH: Yes. It's enough for him that Stephanas is a Greek. The fact that we are both Christians makes no difference—makes matters worse, even!

SOPHIA: Very much worse, I'm afraid. I oughtn't to have said that, perhaps.

JUDITH: Speak freely, please.

SOPHIA: Well, I hate to hurt your feelings, dear, but perhaps I ought to tell you . . . some rather unpleasant stories have been circulating lately—— (JUDITH *winces*.) I'm not saying they're true . . . but they're giving your society a bad name, I'm afraid.

JUDITH (*with a sigh*): And I'm not saying they're *not* true. . . . If you knew all the difficulties we had to contend against, Sophie . . . . Just think what it means—planning a way of life open to all the world—something completely new. . . . We've no traditions behind us, remember.

SOPHIA: Precisely. Because—don't you see, Judy—you've broken away from your traditions . . . traditions that served our ancestors for generations——

JUDITH (*gently*): Don't let us go over all that again, Sophie.

SOPHIA: No. What's the use? (*Dabbing her eyes.*) Oh how I wish we could have remained friends. Do you remember how you used to confide in me—tell me everything about yourself? How I've missed you!

JUDITH (*moved*): I've missed *you*, Sophie. . . . It had to be.

SOPHIA: I sometimes think—I think, for your sake, Judy, I might have become a Christian . . . if it hadn't been for Judah. He's such a good man.

JUDITH: And Stephanas is a good man. (*They are silent for a moment.*) No, I haven't forgotten how I used to confide in you—and what a blessed comfort it was at times. . . . I'm going to confide in you again, if you'll let me. (*Her voice is trembling.*)

SOPHIA: My dear, my dear.

JUDITH: Oh, Sophie, I'm in despair! Perhaps you won't understand. You see, Stephanas lives for this little church of ours—and I live for Stephanas. And after all our pains, to watch it, day by day, just crumbling to pieces. . . . What we've been through! You wouldn't know Stephanas. His hair has turned completely white.

SOPHIA: He's gone to Ephesus, you say?

JUDITH: As a last resort! Our founder, Paul, is working there. Stephanas had gone to consult him. . . . If Paul can't help us, no one can. And I should have had word from Stephanas yesterday. . . . Heaven only knows what may have happened to him. Where Paul is there's always some disturbance. Not long ago he was in prison. Perhaps Stephanas never reached Paul. There was that awful storm the night he sailed. Perhaps—— (*She buries her head against* SOPHIA's *shoulder*).

SOPHIA: Perhaps, on the other hand, Stephanas *has* reached Paul, and perhaps Paul *is* going to help, and perhaps you'll have good news of both of them in the morning.

JUDITH: Thanks. (*She dries her eyes.*) There, I feel better already! . . . I lay awake all night imagining things. You couldn't have chosen a better day for your visit.

SOPHIA: Would you like me to stay the night?

JUDITH: Oh, my dear—you'd be such a godsend! . . . If you won't mind meeting and . . . associating with—— (*She pauses.*)

SOPHIA: With my sister's friends? I'll try not to mind!

JUDITH: And sitting down to table with them? (SOPHIA *is visibly disconcerted.*) I should quite understand, dear . . .

SOPHIA: It's Judah, I was thinking of. . . . Now I'm thinking of you—and I'll risk it !

[JUDITH *presses her hand in gratitude. There is a low treble knock at the street door.*

JUDITH (*rising*): That will be one of them.

[*Enter* CHLOE, *a prematurely aged woman, in agitation.*

CHLOE: Judith !

JUDITH: What is it, Chloe ?

CHLOE (*drawing back*): I thought you'd be alone . . .

JUDITH: You've heard me speak of my sister Sophia ? . . . I've just been pouring out our troubles to her.

CHLOE: Then she won't mind if I——? (*As* SOPHIA *rises.*) No, please don't go. . . . (*To* JUDITH.) Only I wanted to see you before the others come. I promised Melissa.

JUDITH (*to* SOPHIA): Chloe and her daughter Melissa are two of our most devoted workers.

CHLOE: Have you heard anything from Stephanas ?

JUDITH: Not yet. (*Anxiously.*) Is it something new, Chloe ?

CHLOE (*with emotion*): Melissa has been telling me . . . about her uncle.

JUDITH: Brother Sosilas ?

CHLOE (*scornfully*): Brother indeed ! . . . I ought to have warned you against him. I've always really hated him. . . . I know I shouldn't say that, but it's better than lying. One *can't* love really bad people—I mean people who are bad through and through.

JUDITH: Chloe, Chloe ! Can that be said of any one ? Surely there must be some good in your brother, or he'd never have wanted to join us ?

CHLOE: Wait till you hear ! . . . I'd better tell you from the beginning. . . . Sosilas is my only living kinsman. When my husband died, leaving me penniless, with Melissa a babe in arms, this good brother of mine closed his door to us. He'd have let us starve. With God's help, we came through—somehow. It wasn't easy. . . . Then, years afterwards, when Melissa was just fourteen, Sosilas saw us out together—down by the docks, where I was working—and followed us home. He said he'd been trying to find me, to ask forgiveness for his cruelty in the past, and that he wanted to make up for it. So he offered to take Melissa into employment at good wages. Do you know what his business is ?

JUDITH: Doesn't he manage an inn ?

CHLOE: That's what he calls it. Fortunately I discovered in time what sort of an inn it was. He had quite a number of girls working there—earning big money for him: *that* sort of an inn. Melissa was as good looking then as she is now . . .

JUDITH: And such a sweet, gentle soul, Sophie.

CHLOE (*continuing*): It was just after I'd met Priscilla, and been taken to hear Paul preach. So I told Sosilas we didn't need his help. . . . But that didn't put him off. He wanted Melissa, and he knew we were in straits—so he started pestering us with presents—clothes which we badly needed, and food delicacies—and he'd come and talk for hours about Melissa's brilliant prospects . . . the glib-tongued villain ! . . . And sometimes we'd be sorely tempted. But in the end—God be praised—Paul won the battle for us both. . . . After that we thought he'd leave us in peace. He did for a time. Then one day he came to see me again, very humble in his manner, professing that he was worried by a dream he'd had, and begging me to tell him all about our fellowship. And foolishly I took him at his word. It was just before Apollos came to minister here.

JUDITH: I remember your coming to consult me about it.

CHLOE: Do you remember how, at the first prayer-meeting he attended, he . . . spoke with tongues.

[*She shudders at the recollection.* SOPHIE *is puzzled.*

JUDITH: You won't know what that means, Sophie. Some of the brethren experience strange outpourings of the spirit in a state of trance.

SOPHIA: Oh yes. I've heard it can be quite frightening.

JUDITH: Unfortunately the state can be simulated, and it isn't always easy to distinguish between the false and the genuine. (*To* CHLOE.) We all believed Sosilas to be truly inspired.

CHLOE: Yes, and admitted him into our circle on the strength of it. And now—already he's begun to show himself in his true colours ! Would you believe it, sister ?—he has been at his old tricks with Melissa again !

JUDITH: Oh, Chloe ! It isn't possible ?

CHLOE: I found the girl in tears this morning after he'd left her. I'd noticed he'd been rather attentive to her lately. . . . Oh, he's a devil ! Fancy preaching his foul doctrine under the cloak of our blessed Master ! He tells her, sister, that, as re-born Christians, we are free to sin—nay, that the more we sin the more grace we may obtain from repentance !

JUDITH: Horrible ! (*To* SOPHIA.) Now do you see the kind of enemy we have to reckon with ?

SOPHIA: It bears out some of the stories I have heard.

CHLOE: Melissa insisted that I must tell you without delay. She feels that, as we introduced him, we are in a way responsible——

JUDITH: The poor lamb ! We must set her mind at rest on that score at least. But now—how are we to act, Chloe ? Even Stephanas could never quite decide what was the right thing to do. . . . Without Paul's guidance, we are all lost !

CHLOE: Melissa so dreads having to meet her uncle again. She wanted to stay away this evening. I told her she'd be safer in this house than anywhere else, even if he did dare to show himself——

JUDITH: Of course she'll be safe here. You persuaded her to come, I hope ? We all love her so.

[*A young man, pale and thoughtful, has entered from the inner chamber.*

SOPHIA (*rising*): This must be your son. Philip, isn't it ? (*He nods.*) You don't remember your Aunt Sophia ?

PHILIP: I remember Mother took me to see you once. . . . And she has often spoken of you since. (*He kisses her.*)

SOPHIA: What a handsome young man he's grown, Judy ! He'll be wanting to get married soon, I expect !

[PHILIP *abruptly averts his face.* JUDITH *and* CHLOE *look equally embarrassed.*

Forgive me, please, if I've offended . . .

JUDITH: You couldn't know . . .

[*In the ensuing pause there is a treble knock at the street door, and* MELISSA *enters, timidly. She is a beautiful girl, in evident distress.*

PHILIP (*turning eagerly*): Melissa ! (*It is apparent that he is in love with her.*)

MELISSA: Oh, Philip !

[*She stands in the doorway, shy before* SOPHIA.

JUDITH (*going to her*): Come in, dear. Your mother was here before you. . . . (*She kisses her and whispers.*) Be brave—trust in God. . . . (*Leading her forward.*) I want you to meet my sister—and my oldest friend. (MELISSA *inclines her head.*)

PHILIP (*anxiously*): Melissa !

[MELISSA *looks yearningly to him.*

JUDITH: I ought to be seeing to supper. Would you like to help me in the kitchen, Sophie ? (SOPHIA *rises.*)

CHLOE: May I give a hand ?

[*The three women pass into the inner chamber, without further ado.*

PHILIP: Melissa ! No holy kiss to-day ?

MELISSA: I couldn't before a stranger.

PHILIP: But now ? (*They kiss under restraint.*)

MELISSA: Oh, Philip !

PHILIP: What is it, dear ? (*He sits beside her.*)

MELISSA: You didn't hear, then ? Don't ask me to speak of it, now.

PHILIP: Can't I be of help ?

MELISSA: Your presence helps.

PHILIP: My love, you mean. You know that's with you always.

MELISSA: Yes, Philip. But I prefer it with your presence. Is that wicked of me ?

PHILIP (*troubled*): I don't know. Yes, I do. Nothing you may say or think could ever be wicked.

MELISSA: Oh, Philip, you mustn't—you don't know me . . .

PHILIP: Even your tears are beautiful—as if God were shedding love through them.

MELISSA: Oh, I am wicked—full of wickedness. . . . Only don't love me less, Philip—I try so hard to be worthy.

PHILIP: A love like ours can never grow less. It's like the sun.

MELISSA: It keeps me alive, I know that. Oh, but it tortures. God help me !

PHILIP: Melissa ! I'm in torture too. We must be strong, both of us, keep our love high and pure—resist the Devil that is for ever seeking to drag it down.

MELISSA: Sometimes I think it's easier when you're with me. Do you remember that day you asked me to be your spiritual bride ?

PHILIP: Yes, Melissa.

MELISSA: You took my hand.

PHILIP: Yes.

MELISSA: You've never done that since.

PHILIP: Oh, Melissa. (*He takes her hand.*) God forgive me this once !

MELISSA: Philip, if we weren't believers, would you—would you marry me ?

PHILIP: What a question ! Melissa, you aren't weakening in your faith ?

MELISSA: Of course not, Philip. I only wondered . . . (*A pause.*) Philip, I want to tell you something.

PHILIP: Is it what you wouldn't tell me just now?

MELISSA: No, not that.

PHILIP: What is it?

MELISSA: The night before your father left for Ephesus, my mother went to see him.

PHILIP: I know. She gave him a special question to take to Paul. Concerning life after death, was it not?

MELISSA: So she said. I believe it was really about me.

PHILIP: About you? Whatever do you mean?

MELISSA: I don't know what she said. But I know what was in her mind. She's so funny, sometimes. She's been worried about my health. As if Paul could help that!

PHILIP (*all concern*): Your health? Melissa! You are suffering?

MELISSA: Not now, not now. Keep my hand, Philip. Oh, if we could only stay like this for ever!

[*A treble knocking—rather louder than the previous one—and* GLAUCON, *a prosperous business man, enters from the street. He carries a large basket, and is slightly inebriated.* PHILIP *and* MELISSA *have broken apart.*

GLAUCON: Not interrupting, am I? Greetings to you both!

[*They murmur,* " Greetings, Brother Glaucon," *in return.*

I'm a bit early for the feast, I know. Never mind. You're all going to have a taste of something special with me to-night— (*displaying a bottle from his hamper*) all my particular friends, that is. . . . Celebrations! As a matter of fact, I've been celebrating already.

PHILIP: What occasion, Brother Glaucon?

GLAUCON: What, haven't you heard? I won my action!

PHILIP (*sadly*): The case against Brother Artemas, you mean?

GLAUCON (*nodding*): It'll teach our worthy friend not to try and wriggle out of his bargains another time! (*He sits down heavily.*) The whole thing was over in less than an hour—a walk-over! My lawyer knocked the stuffing out of him with his first question. It's what I've always said: a clever lawyer's half the battle. The old judge gave it him hot and strong: " I never heard a feebler defence in the whole course of my experience! Judgment for the Plaintiff for the full amount of his claim, with costs." (*Chuckling, he fails to hear a mechanical treble knocking at the door.*) And seven days to pay it in, or the Defendant goes to jail!

[ARTEMAS, *a less hardened man of the world, has entered in time to catch the last words. He too is carrying a basket.*

ARTEMAS: Sorry to disappoint you, brother, but at least you won't have that satisfaction. The money's already on its way to your lawyer.

GLAUCON (*taken aback*): I didn't see you come in, Brother Artemas. . . . As a matter of fact, I didn't think you'd be coming this evening . . .

ARTEMAS: Quite so, brother. That's why I came. . . . Fortunately, I still have enough money left to fulfil my social obligations. (*He displays his overflowing basket.*) And I've learnt my lesson, don't worry. I'll be careful in future never to have any business dealings with a fellow Christian.

GLAUCON (*uncomfortably*): Business is business, old man.

ARTEMAS: And a dirty trick is a dirty trick, sir.

[PHILIP *and* MELISSA *have been listening with growing dismay.*

PHILIP: Is there nothing I can say or do . . . ? Artemas, Glaucon, in the name of our common brotherhood——

GLAUCON (*with a shrug*): That's all right. The thing's over and done with as far as I'm concerned. I was never one to harbour a grudge. (*Approaching* ARTEMAS.) Kiss and be friends again, eh, Brother Artemas? (*As the latter turns away.*) Just as you please. All one to me.

PHILIP: This is terrible ! . . . as though the air were poisoned.

MELISSA: Oughtn't you to tell your mother?

PHILIP: I suppose so. . . . Poor Mother—on top of all her other troubles. . . .

MELISSA: I'll come with you.

[*They withdraw together into the further room,* ARTEMAS *casually seats himself, and, after an interval,* GLAUCON *follows his example, selecting a chair at an extreme distance. A pause.* GLAUCON *commences to fidget,* ARTEMAS *proceeds to hum.* GLAUCON's *control gives out.*

GLAUCON: Call yourself a Christian !

[ARTEMAS *continues to hum. A treble knock at the street door heralds the entry of* EULALIA, *a massive woman, elaborately attired and veiled. On the threshold she announces solemnly.*

EULALIA: A benediction on all the saints of God here assembled !

[*She deposits a basket on the nearest chair, and proceeds to remove not only her veil, but her headgear, releasing plentiful ringlets of hair—the more conspicuous since the other female characters in the play keep their heads covered throughout.*

GLAUCON *and* ARTEMAS (*murmuring in unison*): Greetings, Sister Eulalia.

EULALIA (*disconcerted*): Is there no one else?

[*A treble knock introducing* LOIS, *an earnest and more simply-garbed woman.*

LOIS: Greetings, all.

[*Murmurs of "Greetings, Sister Lois," equally without warmth.* LOIS *removes her veil and stares with disapproval at* EULALIA, *who, snatching up her basket, crosses the room to seat herself in isolation from the rest of the company. On* LOIS *taking the nearest chair, the four present are seen to be as widely separated as conditions permit. Another strained silence.*

GLAUCON: Papa Stephanas is still abroad on this mysterious mission, I suppose. There's something a bit fishy about it, if you ask me.

ARTEMAS (*snappily*): Nobody asked you.

[JUDITH *returns at that moment, followed by* CHLOE *and* MELISSA, *with* SOPHIA *and* PHILIP *in train. All rise to greet their hostess.*

JUDITH: Welcome, beloved friends. (*Greetings are returned.*) Be seated, please.

[GLAUCON, ARTEMAS, EULALIA *and* LOIS *resume their former seats.*

CHLOE: Come with me, Melissa. (*She takes her to sit, right.* SOPHIA, *feeling rather out of place, has gone to sit, apart, on the opposite side of the room.*)

JUDITH: Philip, will you look after your aunt?

[*Dutifully, he goes to seat himself by* SOPHIA.

EULALIA (*who has been eyeing* SOPHIA): We have a newcomer, I see.

JUDITH: A blood sister of mine, very dear to me. (*Addressing the company.*) I want to say a few words—to make a special appeal to you all—for her sake, if not for mine——

EULALIA: Pardon me, beloved. Your sister is naturally shocked to see a woman's hair uncovered in a mixed assembly. She considers it unwomanly, no doubt. Perhaps I may be allowed to explain myself? (*Some sighing is noticeable. She addresses* SOPHIA.) I claim for Christian women the full liberty of body and soul enjoyed by our male brethren. Are we not children of one father —and, as children, equals? You may tell me that the covering or uncovering of one's head seems to you a trivial matter. I answer that a vital principle is at stake. In refusing to be bound by a degrading social convention I am moved by the same spirit that inspires me to prophetic utterances in our prayer meetings.

It is a spirit that will not be deterred by ridicule or abuse—even by the misunderstanding of my fellows. (*Looking round her.*) One day they will understand—all the world will understand !

LOIS: It is not a question of our understanding or not understanding, sister. It is for us to do as we are advised by our betters. It was laid down quite clearly by Apollos——

EULALIA (*scornfully*): Apollos ! And who is Apollos, to dictate to me on a matter of conscience ? I recognize only one authority in this church: the Apostle Paul.

JUDITH (*who has been vainly signing to them in turn*): Sisters, sisters !

LOIS (*unheeding*): Apollos was established as a preacher, before Paul ever came to Corinth.

EULALIA: Not of the true faith, sister. Remember he had not been properly baptized.

LOIS: Baptism by John was sufficient to make him the most marvellous preacher I was ever privileged to hear. And a great prophet as well. It was a bad day for all of us when he was persuaded to leave Corinth. And the sooner he returns to us the sooner we may expect to see some order restored to this church !

JUDITH (*again interposing*): Sister Lois, I beg of you——

EULALIA (*quietly effective*): And was it by the advice of Apollos, may I ask, that you deserted your lawful husband ?

JUDITH: Now *please*, Eulalia——

LOIS (*calmly*): My husband is not a Christian. That was quite sufficient reason for leaving him.

CHLOE: Forgive me, sister Lois. It was not my intention to reopen that question, but as the subject has been raised, I cannot keep silent. I saw your husband only yesterday. It wrung my heart—the poor man looked utterly broken. And he was always so considerate and so devoted to you——

LOIS (*tight-lipped*): I gave him every chance. He had only to accept our faith. I'm quite sure Apollos would have approved my decision.

EULALIA: Apollos, indeed ! A mere pygmy beside Paul !

[SOSILAS, *a handsome and be-jewelled Greek, has sauntered in, after a perfunctory knocking, in time to take in the last speech.* MELISSA *and* CHLOE, *at sight of him, draw together in apprehension.*

SOSILAS: Bravo, Sister Eulalia ! My sentiments entirely ! Let us be honest for once and admit that, for all his eloquence and learning, the late lamented Apollos was one of the plaguyest bores that ever came out of Egypt—which is saying much ! Paul, present or absent, is the only ruler, for me, of this church—Paul, with his magnificent vitality, his freshness of outlook, his broad-mindedness. Paul, before all things, is a man of the world. As I was explaining to my niece Melissa only this morning—— (*Seeing her.*) Ah, my dear, so you are here before me ! (*He seats himself beside her.*) I hope you have been reflecting on my words ? (*She shrinks from him in disgust.* CHLOE, *supporting her, half rises in protest.*) But the full implications of our faith are perhaps not so easy for the female mind to grasp . . .

MELISSA (*choking*) : I can't stay here . . .

[*She rises abruptly and rushes into the back room.*

PHILIP (*who has been watching with growing concern*) : What is it, Melissa ?

[*He hurries after her.* JUDITH *and* CHLOE *exchange anxious glances.*

JUDITH (*bracing herself to deal with the situation*) : God, give me strength !

[*Again the treble knock at the door, and a party of ill-clad, under-nourished slaves, of both sexes, troops in. They are ill-at-ease.*

MANES (*their spokesman*) : Respectful greetings, on behalf of us all.

JUDITH (*advancing*) : Welcome, friends. Make yourselves at home.

MANES : Thank you kindly, ma'am. We'll be all right here.

[*They shuffle into seats near the door, keeping close together.* GLAUCON *and* LOIS *shift their places to keep apart from them.* SOSILAS *also rises with the same object.*

SOSILAS (*continuing suavely as he moves away*) : As I was remarking, friends, our gospel has an inner significance which is quite beyond the comprehension of a mere pedant like Apollos. Indeed, one would hardly expect to find a just appreciation of its subtle beauty in any mind untutored in the schools of Athens. The marvel to me is that Paul, despite the handicap of his ante-cedents, should have been—as it were, divinely chosen to pro-claim the good news. I regard our Paul as an altogether excep-tional product of this cosmopolitan civilization.

MANES : Begging your pardon, sir, if I might venture to speak——

SOSILAS (*with patronizing condescension*) : Assuredly, my good man.

MANES : Well, did you ever chance to hear the Apostle Peter, sir ?

SOSILAS : I can't say I did.

MANES : Ah, but some of us slave folk have heard him, and what's more, we ain't never likely to forget it. Just a plain ordinary working man he was, sir—a fisherman born and bred—none of your educated scholars, like Paul and Apollos—but he'd known the Master—personally, as you might say—and worked with him right up to the end. . . . And when he spoke to you, it kind of lifted you out of yourself. Some of us would give a lot just to hear that voice again ! (*Murmurs of approval from his comrades.*) So if it's a question of taking sides, and we're allowed any opinion in the matter, Peter's our man ! That's all I wanted to say, sir.

CHLOE: Why must we take sides, brethren ? Why can't we just accept the Master's teaching ?

SOSILAS: All very well, sister, but we must have someone to refer to on points of doubt.

A SLAVE (*in a piping voice*): That's right, sir. We must have a referee.

EULALIA: Someone with a strong personality—like Paul.

LOIS: I don't consider Paul has at all a strong personality. Now, Apollos—— (*General murmuring breaks out.*)

JUDITH (*mustering all her forces*): Beloved, will you let me say one word ? (*There is silence; seats are resumed.*) I had hoped that my dear husband Stephanas would be with us this evening. He has not yet returned from Ephesus. In his absence, won't you all help me, please—show your good will—show forbearance—sink all your differences and resentments—remembering only our common devotion to the Master and Lord. . . . I can say no more.

[*An embarrassed pause.*

GLAUCON: I'm getting hungry, I know that. So what about supper ?

[*A subdued chorus of* " Hear, hear."

ARTEMAS: I have a point to raise about that. This man (*pointing to* GLAUCON) has been attending feasts given by his heathen friends—eating polluted meat. I have evidence of it. Are we to be asked to sit down at the same table with him ?

GLAUCON: There has been no clear ruling against me. Those who don't choose to sit down with me can please themselves. So (*rising*) if supper is ready for us——

JUDITH (*in despair*): Supper is ready for us, but are *we* ready—— ?

[*At that moment* PHILIP *bursts in from the back room, livid.*

PHILIP (*loudly*): Mother ! Melissa has just been telling me—about Sosilas. . . . Will you ask the skunk to leave ?

JUDITH: My son, how *can* I—a fellow churchman—— ?

PHILIP: If you don't, I think—God help me—I am going to kill him !

[*Consternation. Cries of* " Shame," " Brother Philip ! " *etc.*

SOSILAS (*rising, on the defensive*) : You won't find that so easy, young man.

[PHILIP *makes a dash at him, but is restrained by his mother, joined by* CHLOE *and* SOPHIA. EULALIA *and* LOIS *scream.* MELISSA *returns in alarm.*

MELISSA : Philip ! Philip !

[PHILIP *collapses sobbing at his mother's feet.*

JUDITH : Oh God, have mercy on us ! (*She turns to* SOPHIA, *at the end of her resources.*) Sophie ! My faith is giving out . . .

[*Suddenly there is a loud knock at the street door, quite distinct from the previous knocking.*

Chloe, will you see who it is ?

[*Amid a tense silence,* CHLOE *goes to the door and opens it.* TITUS, *a dignified figure, stands without.*

TITUS : Is this the house of Stephanas ?

JUDITH (*in a trembling voice*) : I am his wife.

TITUS (*entering and introducing himself*) : Titus, a brother in the faith, from Ephesus.

JUDITH : Tell me the worst. Stephanas—— ?

TITUS : Is well. He sends loving greetings to you and to his son.

[PHILIP *scrambles to his feet, still shaking violently.* JUDITH *supports him.*

JUDITH : Is he not returning ?

TITUS : Paul has asked him to stay a few days with him.

JUDITH : Paul too is well ?

TITUS : Never better ! And his ministry prospering beyond all expectation, God be praised !

JUDITH : Then he will have no time to spare—— ? Did he not send any message—Paul ?

TITUS : He has given me a letter addressed to the church of Corinth.

JUDITH (*joyfully*) : A letter from Paul himself ! Chloe !

CHLOE : God has heard our prayer !

LOIS (*impatiently*) : Your pardon, Brother Titus. And Apollos ? Is he at Ephesus still ?

TITUS : Yes, sister. He is working with Paul.

LOIS : Is he not coming back to us ? (*Faltering.*) Some of us lately petitioned him . . . privately.

TITUS (*gravely*): He received your petition. Paul strongly urged him to come to you, but Apollos is unwilling. He has heard with grief of things said and done in his name to undermine Paul's authority among you. He will not come to you for that reason.

EULALIA (*with unnecessary fervour*): Praise God for that, too.

JUDITH (*to* TITUS): You must be hungry, brother, after your journey.

TITUS: Thank you. I have eaten. But if I might sit among you . . . ?

JUDITH: May we have Paul's letter ?

TITUS: I was to deliver it into your hands. (*He presents a scroll.*)

JUDITH (*taking it*): Sit at ease, brother. (*He takes a chair.*) Philip ! (*He goes to her.*) Will you read this letter to us ? (*She hands him the scroll.*)

PHILIP (*aghast*): Now ? Oh, Mother——

JUDITH (*peremptorily*): Now ! (*To the company.*) Let us all be seated again. (*She is obeyed, with no great enthusiasm.* MELISSA *now takes a seat beside* CHLOE. SOPHIA *returns to a more isolated position.*) We are ready, Philip.

[PHILIP *masters his emotion after a great effort.*

PHILIP (*in a tremulous voice, reading from the scroll*): " Paul, called to be an apostle of Jesus Christ through the will of God unto the Church of God which is at Corinth . . . "

[*The curtain descends to mark an interval of time. When it rises again,* PHILIP *is concluding his reading of the letter. There is a marked change in the atmosphere. Except for* SOSILAS, *who remains cool and detached, bored and sullen looks have given way to expressions uniformly tense and reverential. Many are in tears or on their knees.* PHILIP'S *voice has acquired strength and resonance.*

" I, Paul, add this salutation in my own hand. If any man love not the Lord let him be anathema. The grace of our Lord Jesus Christ be with you. And my love be with you all."

[*The hand holding the scroll drops to his side. There is a chorus of* " Amen." *No one stirs for some moments.*

JUDITH (*quietly*): Thank you, Philip. Will you give me the letter. (*He hands it back to her. She examines it, much moved.*) It is in your father's handwriting. (*He nods.*) Paul must have dictated it to him —all but the last sentence.

[PHILIP *suddenly drops to his knees, buries his head in his hands.*

MELISSA (*to* CHLOE, *in a whisper*) : Mother ! That part about marriage. . . . You must have told him—of Philip and me !

CHLOE : And if I did ? (*Aloud.*) What were Paul's words about us ? " Not many wise, not many mighty, not many noble " . . . but we have been called, and we are his children. Let us give thanks for such a father, even when he chides us. (*Murmurs of assent.*)

MANES (*on his knees*) : I am so ashamed of my presumption !

[*On an impulse*, LOIS *rises.*

LOIS (*unsteadily*) : I can't stay now. I am going back—to my husband. . . . Forgive me, brethren.

JUDITH (*going with her to the door*) : We understand, sister. (*She kisses her.*)

LOIS : I'll be with you all at to-morrow's meeting.

[*She adjusts her veil, and* JUDITH *lets her out.*

ARTEMAS (*on his knees*) : Brother Glaucon, I have been hating you in my heart. Will you forgive me ?

GLAUCON (*with a cry*) : Brother, but I wronged you. It is for me to ask forgiveness. The money will be returned to you.

ARTEMAS : No, no, brother, I made the bargain. I should have kept to it.

GLAUCON : It was no honest bargain. I abused your trust in me. How can I keep the money ?

ARTEMAS : Let us give it to the saints' fund.

GLAUCON : If only I may have your love again.

ARTEMAS : With all my heart, brother.

[*He goes across to him, and they embrace.*

SOSILAS (*rising with great complacency*) : Love—ah, what a comprehensive word ! And how brilliantly elucidated by our spiritual father ! Love, as he puts it, " suffereth all things, taketh not account of evil." Did you mark those words, Melissa ?

[PHILIP *has risen, but retains full control of himself.*

JUDITH (*in a clear, firm voice*) : Sosilas, will you leave this house at once !

SOSILAS (*taken aback*) : What ? Expel me from the church, would you ? By what right ? (*She holds up* PAUL's *letter.*) I see. So that is how you understand the Apostle's message ? (*With a shrug.*) Well, you should know him better than I perhaps ! (*Dropping the mask.*) Paul, Apollos, Peter, the great risen Messiah—shall I tell you what they are, one and all ? (*He snaps his fingers.*) Just a lot of swinish Jews ! They can't fool me ! As for my weak-minded sister and her sentimental chit of a daughter, if they want to throw their lives away, I'll not lift a finger for them again ! I wash my hands of the lot of you !

[*Snorting contempt, he marches out, slamming the door behind him.*

MELISSA (*catching* PHILIP's *eye*) : It's as though I could breathe at last !

[EULALIA *is now seen to be replacing her headgear.*

EULALIA (*between sobs*) : I wouldn't do it for anyone but Paul !— And I shall never open my lips at a prayer meeting again. . . . (*She struggles to control her emotion.*) If Paul says its wrong, that's enough for me. . . . But it isn't wrong, it *can't* be . . . Paul's more important, that's all. I'd go through fire for Paul !

MANES (*fervently*) : We all would, sister. (CHLOE *has gone to comfort* EULALIA.)

JUDITH : Shall we hold our love-feast now ? (*General assent. Only* MELISSA *and* PHILIP *remain absorbed in each other.*) Brother Titus ? (*She signs to him to lead the way.*)

GLAUCON (*offering his basket to her*) : Will you accept this for the common stock, sister ?

ARTEMAS (*following suit*) : Mine too !

JUDITH : Will you take them, Brother Manes ? (*He obeys.*) Come, dear friends.

[*She conducts the slaves, following* TITUS *into the back room.* CHLOE *follows, supporting* EULALIA. *Then* GLAUCON *and* ARTEMAS, *arm in arm.* SOPHIA *remains unnoticed in her corner seat.* MELISSA *slowly approaches* PHILIP, *their eyes still holding together.*

PHILIP (*softly*) : Melissa !

MELISSA (*in a whisper*) : " Let him marry her."

PHILIP (*looking away*) : I might have committed murder.

MELISSA : I might never have met you.

PHILIP : Oh, Melissa ! (*Her arms are about him.*) What a fool you're marrying ! (*He clasps her to him.*)

MELISSA : Just a pair of fools, aren't we ?

[*Still embracing, they move slowly through the centre door.* SOPHIA *is now alone. She rises, stands irresolute for a moment, then steals across to the street door.* JUDITH's *voice arrests her.*

JUDITH : Sophie ! (*She comes quickly in, looking anxiously about her.*) Sophie ! (*She sees her.*) You were going away ! Did you think I'd forgotten you ?

SOPHIA : I wasn't blaming you.

JUDITH: Oh, my heart is so full ! But you said you'd stay ?

SOPHIA: You don't need me now.

JUDITH: Wasn't it wonderful, Sophie ! And to think I nearly lost faith. I can never, never doubt again. . . . Won't you remain just the same, dear ?

SOPHIA: I can't. Don't you see, it makes all the difference. It would be like treachery to Judah. . . . " As God hath called each, so let him walk." That was Paul's message to me. . . . You must go back to your guests. (*She opens the door.*)

JUDITH: Our church has come to stay, Sophie.

SOPHIA: I know that. With faith, hope and love, how could it be otherwise ? Perhaps I am a little jealous of you. (*She kisses her.*) Will you remember your elder sister sometimes, in your prayers ?

[*She breaks away, veils herself, and goes quickly out into the night.* JUDITH *goes thoughtfully to join the love-feast.*

CURTAIN

NOTE

To read the Bible, *à la mode,* " as literature " is at any rate to read the Bible; to study it as an " inspired " record of religious experiences is an exercise which many people are finding more appropriate to the times in which we live. Readers of this play who are familiar with " The First Epistle of Paul the Apostle to the Corinthians," from either standpoint, will notice that two of my characters have been " lifted " straight out of that document—Chloe (i. 11) and the absent Stephanas (i. 16, xvi. 15–18). The rôle of Titus, as bearer of the letter, has been inferred from passages outside the Epistle itself. Most of the other characters, imagined by me as to form and name, will be recognized, however vaguely, by " religious " (as distinct from literary) students, as the individuals, brothers and sisters in the spirit, whose personal difficulties are evoked with so many vivid touches in the practical directions forming the bones of the letter. Thus—to give chapter and verse—the party-politicians of the Church (" I am for Paul "; " I for Apollos "; " I for Peter ") are reproved in i. 10–17, and again in iv. 6; the dilemma of Philip and Melissa is conjured up in vii. 25–30 (adopting Moffatt's " spiritual bride " for the " virgin " of the A.V. and " virgin daughter " of the R.V.) ; Glaucon and Artemas are corrected in vi. 1–11: Eulalia is the unfortunate " Aunt Sally " of xi. 3–16; Lois is restored to her husband in vii. 13. Sosilas may stand for the type of immoralist whose expulsion from the Church is commanded in Chapter V. The only character for whom there is no specific Scriptural warrant is the non-" Christian " Sophia. May I be pardoned for believing—as I do—that she is none the less true, historically.

Of the great spiritual message, summed up in Chapter XIII of the Epistle, it would not become me to say more than that I am profoundly conscious of my inability adequately to communicate it in another medium.

HOLYEST ERTH

" Sothely Glastenbury is the holyest erth of england."—From *The Lyfe of Joseph of Armathia* (a poem printed in 1520), Early English Text Society, No. 44.

CHARACTERS

ARVIRAGUS, a Druid priest
MATUNA, his wife
CORDEL, their daughter-in-law
SULI ⎫ Cordel's children
BRAN ⎭
JOSEPH OF ARIMATHEA

Scene: At the foot of Glastonbury Tor
Time: Autumn, A.D. 61

An ancient well, now enclosed in private property, belonged, with the rounded, grassy height rising immediately north-east of it (now known as Glastonbury Tor), to the Island of Avalon, in the days when sea-water, flowing in from the Bristol Channel, covered most of the land between the Mendip and the Quantock Hills. That well is in the centre of the stage and, obliquely, on the right, a hut with thatched roof screens us from the green slopes of the familiar landmark. Apart from the door of the house, two stage entrances will be employed: one from the corner of the right and rear representing a path descending from the Tor, the other, front left as leading to the extremity of the isle crowned by the sister height now called Weary-all Hill. Three or four stools are set before the hut and on one of these MATUNA, *an elderly woman, sits gazing out towards the sun and the sea (in the " fourth wall " of the stage) erect and dry-eyed in grief.* SULI, *a girl of thirteen, descending from the Tor, emerges from the entrance on the right. She carries a basket filled with apples.*

SULI: Granny ! (*Raising her voice.*) Grandma !

MATUNA (*without looking at her*): Yes, Suli ?

SULI (*timidly*): Is Mum still indoors ?

MATUNA (*nodding*): I have just left her. Where have you been, child ?

SULI: Only picking apples. (*She puts the basket down by the door.*) Granny, why has Mummy been crying ?

MATUNA: Hasn't she told you anything ? (SULI *shakes her head.*) We have had bad news.

SULI: Of a battle ? (MATUNA *nods.*) The Romans have beaten us, I suppose.

MATUNA: I'm afraid so.

SULI (*advancing a step*) : Have—have they killed my Daddy ?

MATUNA : Yes, my poor lamb—with many, many other brave men.

SULI : Oh, Granny ! (*She whispers a little.*) Does my brother know ?

MATUNA : Mummy told him last night.

SULI (*looking round*) : Where is he now ?

MATUNA : Bran will be back presently, I expect. . . . Come, Suli. (*She takes her in her arms.*) I know, I know, love. We can only try to be brave.

SULI : I will try. (*Breaking away.*) Where was the battle fought, Granny ?

MATUNA : Over in Mona.

SULI : Is that the island with the old oak grove that Grandpa loves so ?

MATUNA : The grove has been utterly destroyed.

SULI : Grandma, oh, oh. . . .

MATUNA (*with restraint*) : Have you seen your grandfather ?

SULI : He passed me on his way up to the sanctuary.

MATUNA : I thought he would be there.

SULI : Grandma. (*She brings the other stool nearer, and seats herself on it.*)

MATUNA : Yes, dearie.

SULI : Will the Romans come to Avalon now ?

MATUNA : They may.

SULI : Then we shall all be killed ? (MATUNA *doesn't answer.*) Why do they hate us so, Granny ?

MATUNA : Because they know that we shall never submit to them —never, never !

SULI : The people of Gaul submitted.

MATUNA : Those who weren't killed or who didn't escape to Britain.

SULI : Many of our people have submitted, too, haven't they ?

MATUNA : *Our* people ?

SULI : The people of Britain.

MATUNA : Kings of Britain have submitted and their subjects with them. We owe no allegiance to such kings. There are kings of a different kind. Your grandfather is one.

SULI : But we are people of Britain all the same, aren't we, Grandma ?

MATUNA: We are Druids of Britain. To submit to Rome would be for us to betray a trust. We would die rather than do that.

SULI (*subdued*): Here comes Grandfather.

[*Enter, from the right,* ARVIRAGUS, *in the flowing white robe of a Druid priest, leaning somewhat heavily on his staff; grave but composed.*

MATUNA (*rising*): I have told the child, Arviragus.

ARVIRAGUS: Best so. (*Looking around.*) Has Bran not returned yet?

MATUNA: I haven't seen him. Have you, Suli? (*As* SULI *shakes her head.*) He is staying for later news perhaps. Or—— (*Suddenly panicking.*) I don't know what to think. Is it possible the Romans already—from Caerleon perhaps——?

ARVIRAGUS: It is not possible. (*He takes her hand, holding it between his own.*) All has been quiet?

MATUNA (*less agitated*): Morgen has gone—with his family——

ARVIRAGUS (*calmly as ever*): We may see them again.

MATUNA: You are sure it is right for us to keep the children here?

ARVIRAGUS: No less right than before.

MATUNA: We are the only ones left now.

ARVIRAGUS (*with a smile*): What! Has even old Camul deserted us? (*He releases her hand.*)

SULI: He was sitting in his boat as usual when I left the Haven—hardly an hour ago.

MATUNA: If you count a poor daft fisherman!

SULI: He looked dafter than ever to-day! He was sitting bolt upright just as if he was listening for something.

MATUNA: There has been a strange lull in the air all day.

SULI: I noticed it too, Grandma.

ARVIRAGUS: There is always a strangeness in the air of Avalon.

MATUNA: I never knew it like this before.

ARVIRAGUS: No. It is something new.

[*Enter from the house,* CORDEL, *his daughter-in-law, Suli's mother, a woman in the early thirties. Her eyes are swollen from weeping.*

CORDEL (*advancing with set mouth*): Suli! Where's Bran?

SULI: He isn't back yet. (*Her voice breaking.*) Oh, Mummy, I—I know. (*She runs into her arms.*)

CORDEL: Did Granny tell you? I was too cowardly! (*Clasping her tight.*) We shall see him again. Never forget that. Anything else isn't possible. Daddy's father knows. (*Looking at him.*) Tell her, will you?

ARVIRAGUS: Yes, I know, Suli. Nothing ends in that way.

CORDEL: I believe it! If only—if only, Father, I could hear his laugh again, his dear laugh—just this once! (SULI *gives a sob.*) I shouldn't have said that, Suli darling. We mustn't weaken—any of us. (*Breaking away.*) Are you sure Bran isn't back?

MATUNA: Not unless he returned before I came out. . . . Don't worry, dear. He can look after himself.

CORDEL: You saw him last, Suli. Did he say anything when you went off together?

SULI: He hardly opened his mouth. I couldn't think why. *Now* I know.

CORDEL: If he hasn't left the mainland by now, he'll have missed the tide.

MATUNA (*to* ARVIRAGUS): Did you happen to look out to sea when you were up there? (*Indicating the Tor.*)

ARVIRAGUS: The mist had come up again. It covered everything —except for a break, over towards our sister mount. (*He hesitates.*) I don't think I saw anything that was really there.

MATUNA: What did you think you had seen?

ARVIRAGUS (*slowly*): A foreign ship. It was standing a little out from the Haven, with Camul's boat pulling away from it. The next moment the mist had closed in.

MATUNA: How long ago was this?

ARVIRAGUS: Quite an hour, I should say. I wasn't paying much heed. It was a day-dream, I think.

CORDEL: Unless it was a Roman ship. It wouldn't surprise me if they'd sent a patrol on our track.

ARVIRAGUS (*quietly*): If so, there is nothing any of us can do. We are alone here on this island.

CORDEL: If only Bran were back!

SULI (*sharp-eared*): There's someone coming. I heard a foot stumble.

MATUNA: The mist is rising all round again.

SULI: No, it can't be Bran, Mother. It's someone quite old, I think.

CORDEL: Don't trust any stranger. He may be a spy.

[*A stranger enters, on her words, from the left. It is* JOSEPH OF ARIMATHEA, *old and exhausted, peering before him as he advances unsteadily, lacking a staff, under a pack strapped over his shoulders.*

JOSEPH: Pardon. (*Pointing.*) Is that not a well?

ARVIRAGUS: You want a drink?

JOSEPH: If I might fill my water bottle . . . (*He takes it from his girdle.*)

ARVIRAGUS: The well is not in use at present. Fetch some water from the house, Suli.

JOSEPH (*as* SULI *stands eyeing him suspiciously*): Perhaps she will take the bottle?

[SULI *almost snatches it from him and goes into the house angrily.*

MATUNA: Won't you sit down? (*She brings a stool forward.*)

JOSEPH: Thank you. (*He lowers himself on to the stool.*) My staff unfortunately stuck fast in the marshy ground as I landed.

MATUNA: Wouldn't you like to remove your pack?

JOSEPH: Not yet.

[SULI *returns from the house with his water bottle, but remains at a distance.*

CORDEL: Give the man his water bottle, Suli.

[*She advances unwillingly.*

JOSEPH: She is afraid of me, I think. (*Addressing her.*) Do you understand my speech?

SULI: Yes. You are a Roman, aren't you?

JOSEPH: A Roman? I? No, my dear. (*She returns him his water bottle.*) Thank you. (*He drinks.*)

SULI (*bluntly*): Why have you come here?

JOSEPH: Yes. It is natural that you should want to know that. I don't think I can explain. (*He half rises.*) Perhaps I had better be going now.

ARVIRAGUS (*gently*): Where do you think you are going to? (JOSEPH *stares about him.*) We are the only inhabitants left upon this island. You have reached your journey's end, it seems.

MATUNA: Wouldn't you like something to eat?

JOSEPH: Thank you, but I may not eat before sundown.

SULI: Why not?

JOSEPH: Because—because, my little maid, this happens to be the tenth day of the seventh month of the year, and I can't forget it. (*With a smile.*) Have you ever found yourself trying to forget something you just can't help remembering? (*She doesn't answer.*) She is still frightened of me.

MATUNA: The child has had a great shock.

JOSEPH: You call her Suli, I think. (*Turning to her.*) Do you like stories, Suli? (*She nods.*) I will tell you the story of a man called Jonah who tried his hardest to forget something he had to remember. (*She draws closer.*) He went on a long sea voyage to take him as far as possible away from the thing he wanted to forget. But a great storm broke out and, of course, that brought it all back to him, and made him very unhappy. So he begged the captain to throw him overboard: he thought if he were drowned he'd be sure to forget. Well, they did throw him overboard, but—what do you think?—a great fish came along and swallowed poor Jonah right up! For three days and three nights he lived inside that fish. And then the fish spewed him up on to dry land again. And then, of course, he remembered again. Wasn't it annoying?

SULI (*more friendly*): What was it he wanted to forget?

JOSEPH: It was a message he had to take to some people in a strange land.

SULI: Is your name Jonah?

JOSEPH: No. My name is Joseph. Do you like the name?

SULI: It's all right. . . . When did you last have something to eat?

[JOSEPH *suddenly buries his face in his hands.*

CORDEL (*to* SULI): You shouldn't be asking so many questions, dear. You can see how tired he is.

JOSEPH (*raising his head, and passing his hand over his brow*): No, I am not tired. But I think I am asleep and dreaming. (*Trying to work it out in his mind.*) I had no intention of coming here. We seemed to be sailing into a mist. Suddenly it cleared in front of me, and I saw the outline of a hill. . . . I think I must have asked if I could be landed. There was a small boat putting out from shore. The boatman was rowing in our direction, almost within hailing distance.

SULI: Old Camul!

ARVIRAGUS: So my eyes did not deceive me!

JOSEPH: I remember stepping ashore at the foot of a hill, and climbing to the top of it. But it wasn't the hill I wanted. *Then* I felt tired, so I rested there awhile. Afterwards I started to look for the other hill, the hill I saw from the ship.

ARVIRAGUS: We call it the Tor. It is just behind you. (JOSEPH *rises to follow his indication.*) The mist is lifting a little.

JOSEPH (*his back to the audience*): Yes. I can see the slope distinctly now. (*Quite simply.*) I would like to end my days here. (*Turning to* ARVIRAGUS.) Is there a place where I might lay my head in peace?

ARVIRAGUS: Our hut is one of twelve encircling the mount. The others are untenanted; you will be welcome as a neighbour. (JOSEPH *bows low*.) My name is Arviragus. (*Presenting them in turn*.) This is my wife, Matuna, Cordel, our daughter-in-law, Suli you know already.

MATUNA: The hut nearest to ours was vacated only to-day.

SULI (*to her mother*): May I go and make it ready for him?

CORDEL: If you like. (*With a smile to* JOSEPH, SULI *runs off, right, at once*.)

MATUNA: You will at last remove your pack, I hope.

JOSEPH: Not yet. (*Vaguely*.) Presently, perhaps.

CORDEL (*with a last trace of suspicion*): You come as a friend, we are sure.

JOSEPH: How else should one come to so peaceful a homestead, in so gracious a land?

CORDEL: The Romans may come—to kill us. That is why the others have fled.

JOSEPH: I had forgotten the Romans. And Suli thought I was one of them! Well, one stranger is like another.

ARVIRAGUS: You come from afar? (*He nods*.) From some Eastern kingdom?

MATUNA: From a land not ruled by Rome, perhaps?

JOSEPH: From a Roman Province, yet not wholly ruled; from a nation that keeps its faith inviolate.

ARVIRAGUS: You should feel at home among us, in that case.

JOSEPH: I have felt so from the first. (*Dreamily*.) I was born in a hill-town, in a land of hills.

ARVIRAGUS (*solemnly*): This is a holy hill.

JOSEPH: The land I come from is a holy land.

[*A pause of some duration.*

MATUNA (*suddenly*): The mist has quite lifted now.

CORDEL (*anxious again*): And no sign of Bran yet! What can have happened to him? I am doing down to the Haven. Camul may have seen something. (*Her voice breaking*.) If he doesn't come back soon I—I—— (*She stumbles off, left*.)

MATUNA (*to* JOSEPH): Bran is her son. She is newly widowed.

JOSEPH: Alas!

ARVIRAGUS (*whose gaze has never left him*): Your pardon, sir, but this hill-town of which you spoke——

JOSEPH: It is called Arimathea.

ARVIRAGUS: In the land of Judea, I think? You are an Israelite?

JOSEPH: You have heard of Israel?

ARVIRAGUS: From a trader who visited your chief city and told of a great temple there.

JOSEPH: I used to worship in that temple.

ARVIRAGUS: You are a priest?

JOSEPH: Not I, sir.

ARVIRAGUS: I am one. Of a cult that worships, not in temples, but in sanctuaries open to the sun. Like your nation, we acknowledge one God only, Creator and Lord of all things. You seem surprised.

JOSEPH: I had thought you Britons were heathen folk.

ARVIRAGUS: Heathen is your name for those who worship many gods? (*As* JOSEPH *nods.*) Most inhabitants of Britain are heathen. We Druids live separate from the mass of our fellow men. We are not permitted to impart our knowledge outside the circle of our schools. I may tell you that we are endowed with certain powers. Some of us are adept in the second sight. I myself have learnt by prevision much that is now happening in the outer world. In like manner, although uncertain of the day and time, I expected your coming here.

JOSEPH: You tell me marvels!

ARVIRAGUS: If I see truly, you have greater marvels to tell us. . . . (*As* JOSEPH *stares back at him.*) Matuna, you will be preparing for supper. Our visitor will join us, I hope.

MATUNA (*to* JOSEPH, *as taking the hint, she moves towards the house*): You would refrain from eating till then?

JOSEPH: Until sundown. Then, gladly at your table.

[MATUNA *leaves them.*

ARVIRAGUS: It is a day of observance with you?

JOSEPH: The most solemn of all: the Day of Atonement.

[*At the recollection, he bows his head, praying silently. Abruptly, he looks up and glances enquiringly at* ARVIRAGUS.

ARVIRAGUS: You have a question to ask?

JOSEPH: Yes. How do you bury your dead?

ARVIRAGUS: In the earth, with simple rites. . . . (*The other's lips twist wryly.*) You smile?

126

JOSEPH: At the vainglory of human ambition. In the days of my prosperity I used to picture to myself the crowning ceremony of a distinguished career: a funeral with all Jerusalem attending to pay their last respects. I even appointed a resting-place for my honoured remains. I purchased with a great sum of money a noble tomb cut in a rock. (*His voice dies away as a fit of trembling seizes him.*)

ARVIRAGUS (*standing before him*): Joseph, my friend ! Why will you not lay your pack aside ? (*As he does not answer.*) There is a burden on your soul, I think ?

JOSEPH (*in a low voice*): A burden—and no atonement.

ARVIRAGUS: Atonement means to be at one with God, I think ?

JOSEPH: You understand even that ?

ARVIRAGUS: Yet you will not confide in me ? (*As* JOSEPH *turns away.*) Then, if you will permit, I must confide in you, for I, too, am troubled at heart.

JOSEPH (*gently*): You have suffered bereavement. I should have condoled.

ARVIRAGUS: I do not speak of private grief. I am oppressed with the cares of an office, shared in the past with others, of whom, I greatly fear, none are now left alive. In ways which may not be divulged, we have ministered to these islanders—to the people of Britain, I mean—faithful to a sacred charge laid upon our fathers.* [You may wonder at such a charge, esteeming these Britons to be no better than other barbarians. And now let me ask you a question. Can you understand that the God we worship might in his infinite wisdom have chosen to mingle a dozen rude tribes wherefrom to fashion a single united nation ?

JOSEPH (*blinking*): Chosen—a dozen tribes, you say ?

ARVIRAGUS: And designed for the nation composed of those mingled tribes a mission for the blessing of all other nations ? Can you believe in the possibility ?

JOSEPH: In truth, I can !

ARVIRAGUS (*gazing into space-time*): I believe that a British nation is destined to establish an empire mighty beyond even the dreams of Rome.

JOSEPH: Is this by your gift of second sight ?

ARVIRAGUS: By that or of madness, is it not ? But that is not all. I apprehend that in this glory reserved for a British nation, we Druids are to have no part.] Our task has been to prepare the

* The passage in square brackets may be omitted in performance, if desired.

soil: others are needed to till it. It is a good soil for the sower of good seed. (*Looking hard at him.*) Have my words a meaning for you?

JOSEPH: A confused meaning.

ARVIRAGUS: It will suffice. And now, instruct me, I pray, in the ways of Israel—a people set apart—am I not right?—by the same divine providence.

JOSEPH: What would you know of us? Where am I to begin?

ARVIRAGUS: Will you begin with the Day of Atonement? (*Leaning forward earnestly.*) Tell me, by what method is atonement achieved in your community?

JOSEPH: By sacrifice, cleansing us from our sins.

ARVIRAGUS: Offerings on an altar?

JOSEPH: Our fathers offered animals, and the rite still holds its place in our temple service. But, generations back, our Prophet Isaiah denounced the sacrifice of animals as an abomination to the Most High.

ARVIRAGUS: Greater abomination alas! has stained our worship!

JOSEPH: It has been taught that in the shedding of the blood we may find a pattern of the true sacrifice required by God.

ARVIRAGUS: The true sacrifice—that is what I would learn of you.

JOSEPH: Long before Isaiah, the Prophet Amos commanded in God's name: "I will have mercy and not sacrifice."

ARVIRAGUS: Ah. . . . These Prophets of yours—they are mouthpieces of God?

JOSEPH: No less.

ARVIRAGUS: Are such men of God still among you?

JOSEPH (*slowly*): I have known one—yet not like those of former times. (*He pauses.*) He was more than a man. He was without sin. He loved as God loves.

ARVIRAGUS (*rising, with outstretched arms*): It is the word I have been awaiting!

[*At that moment* MATUNA *emerges from the house, one hand clutching a coloured scarf, the other over her heart.*

ARVIRAGUS (*hastening to her side*): My dearest! What is it? (JOSEPH *has risen.*)

MATUNA (*half-drawing back*): Nothing. Take no notice! It was only—— (*She raises the scarf.*) I found it by chance——

ARVIRAGUS (*to* JOSEPH, *as he takes it*): It belonged to our son. He died in battle.

128

MATUNA (*unable to stem her tears*): I keep reproaching myself—I can't help it. If we had gone with the others—I might have been with him at the end——

ARVIRAGUS (*his arm over her shoulder*): Would it have helped, Matuna?

MATUNA: Maybe not. Yet—only to have been with him—even to have seen him suffering. And to think of his poor broken body left untended—unburied, perhaps! . . . (*Regaining composure.*) May I have it back? (*She takes the scarf again, then turns to* JOSEPH.) He was quite a young man—in his thirties. . . It pierces like a sword here. (*Pressing her heart.*)

JOSEPH (*averting his eyes*): That echo. . . . You speak for every mother, I think.

ARVIRAGUS (*as she turns to go*): Wait, Matuna. (*She stops.*) Our guest has brought word of one, more than a man.

MATUNA (*awestruck*): So the voices spoke truly!

ARVIRAGUS (*to* JOSEPH): May we know his name?

JOSEPH: The name is Jesus. He was a village carpenter.

MATUNA: And now—your High Priest?

JOSEPH (*shaking his head*): Our High Priest was his enemy.

ARVIRAGUS: Was? Jesus—is he not alive now?

JOSEPH: The Romans killed him.

MATUNA: Him too? Was it in battle?

JOSEPH: Not in battle. His teaching forbade opposing Roman arms. Many hated him for that.

MATUNA: His teaching reached Avalon, I think. Arviragus insisted that Rome was not to be conquered that way. The Brethren would not listen. Many reproached us for standing aside. Our son went with them, respecting our motive, as we honoured his. (*Intensely.*) Rome will yet fall.

JOSEPH: In God's time.

ARVIRAGUS: In God's way.

MATUNA (*after a pause*): So they put Jesus to death?

JOSEPH: And he prayed that his enemies might be forgiven, " for they know not what they do." He was hanging nailed to a cross when he spoke those words.

MATUNA: Had he lived long?

JOSEPH: He was a little younger than your son. And his mother was standing by the cross till the end. (MATUNA *covers her eyes.*) She would not leave. (*Raising his fists in protest.*) Yes—it was horrible!

EH

ARVIRAGUS: You yourself were present, then?

MATUNA: Did his body receive burial?

JOSEPH (*after a pause*): It was laid in a tomb cut out of a rock.

ARVIRAGUS: The tomb you had purchased for your own burial?

JOSEPH (*in a grim whisper*): The tomb that is now empty.

ARVIRAGUS: Empty?

MATUNA: I do not understand——

JOSEPH (*harshly*): I did not ask you to understand. I stated a fact. As for the burial (*his voice rising*), it was known to all Jerusalem that the body was laid in my tomb.

MATUNA (*soothingly*): He had a faithful friend in you.

JOSEPH (*with suppressed violence*): He had twelve friends. One betrayed him, and the others ran away when the blow fell. I was not of the twelve. I was a Councillor, a man of wealth and dignity, ashamed to associate with my inferiors. But all my life, in my heart, I had been waiting for the kingdom, and once in the Temple I had stayed to hear him teaching. . . . and after that it was never the same. And so—though I was not his friend—I had to do what could be done to avert the infamy . . . when it was too late! (*With increasing agitation.*) And I had to drag my feet up that hill to see him writhing in agony, and to see his mother watching . . . (*Some moments elapse before he can continue.*) A man of my own class, a ruler of the synagogue, who had received the teaching secretly, stood by my side. (*Crescendo.*) To hear that mother pleading for the body, and the ruffians answering that they didn't take orders from Jewish vermin, was more than either of us could stand. So together we went to the Palace, and grovelled before the Roman Governor, the man of blood, till we had his order for the body to be handed to us for burial. (*He pauses.*) And my own precious tomb was close at hand. (*His voice sinks to a whisper.*) What was done that night never seemed real to me afterwards.

ARVIRAGUS: You speak of events long past?

JOSEPH: I have endured thirty Days of Atonement since.

ARVIRAGUS: And in those thirty years the crucified One has not been forgotten?

JOSEPH: Forgotten! When already within a week of his burial he—— (*He checks himself.*)

MATUNA (*eagerly*): Yes? What happened?

JOSEPH: His followers reported that he had appeared to them.

MATUNA: Appeared to them? After his burial?

JOSEPH (*averting his face, hurriedly*): Appeared in the flesh! Later they saw him ascend into Heaven. . . . They were truthful witnesses. They have proclaimed the news not only in Judea, but in countless places abroad, even in Rome. And everywhere fierce quarrels rage between those who acknowledge, and those who will not or cannot accept the doctrine.

ARVIRAGUS (*steadily*): What doctrine?

JOSEPH: Do not ask me that! In Jerusalem it is one thing, in Antioch another, in Alexandria something quite different—and always, everywhere it is changing, changing. . . . How am I to explain when I cannot even understand it? (*He groans.*) Is it not enough that he was what he was? (*Distractedly.*) But it was he and no other they declare they saw: the Risen Lord! And they were honest witnesses, every one of them.

MATUNA (*hardly listening*): The Risen Lord! Arviragus—— (*Turning to him.*)

ARVIRAGUS: Yes, the Appointed One, the Saviour for whom the whole world has been waiting.

JOSEPH (*in despair*): You say that too. Everywhere it is the same! It has only to be told that one who was crucified has risen again: that is enough. (*Vehemently.*) I say it is his teaching, and his example and his spirit—the faithfulness and the wonder of his love so long as a breath remained in him—I say it is these things that matter! What if there had been no resurrection—if his broken body were still lying in that tomb—or in any other tomb? Still I say he would be our King, our Messiah!

ARVIRAGUS (*quietly, as before*): Yet, in truth, that body was seen, you tell us?

JOSEPH: By not one, but several of the Brethren—eyewitnesses of unimpeachable honesty! On the morning of the third day, already before dawn, women had come to the tomb and found it empty. The heavy stone that sealed it had been rolled aside. Afterwards he appeared to these women, and to other followers.

ARVIRAGUS: In their visions?

JOSEPH: He spoke with them. He ate with some. One he suffered to touch his side. To more and more of them he appeared as days and weeks went by; to a company of some hundreds—to his own brother who had scorned him before he died, to the Apostle Paul who had never seen him before.

ARVIRAGUS (*quietly as ever*): To me also in this island.

JOSEPH (*recoiling*) : What are you saying ? To you ? He appeared ?
ARVIRAGUS: Does that seem to you stranger than the other appearances ?

JOSEPH (*wildly*) : Stranger ? You are right ! It is no whit stranger. If his physical body had not risen from the tomb, he could have appeared to no one.

ARVIRAGUS (*looking searchingly at him*) : Why are you keeping something back ? Here in Avalon, truth may be spoken freely.

JOSEPH (*surrendering*) : Then I will tell you the truth. (*With an immense effort.*) There was no resurrection. I know the body did not rise from that tomb. I myself—with the help of a servant—removed it overnight to another tomb.

ARVIRAGUS (*impassively as ever*) : Why did you do it ?

JOSEPH: For the worst of reasons ! It was my accursed pride ! A crucified carpenter was not good enough for my sepulchre ! (*Agony alternating with relief, as after an abscess has burst.*) Before the stone had closed the tomb, I was already repenting my sacrifice, and meanly contriving the second burial. It was not my intention to deceive. My servant was to have returned to the garden at daybreak to direct the mourners to an inconspicuous grave close by. He came too late. The women were there first, had left hurriedly, and were starting the rumour that the body had risen. If I had only spoken when the report reached me——! But I hesitated—from shame, added to confusion of thought and weariness. . . . The opportunity never came again. The rumour was spreading like lightning, and with each day's delay the consequences became more momentous. To have disclosed my secret would have been to stifle a new-born hope to which those poor stricken men and women were clinging in dependence—more, it would have discredited them, and, with them, a Way towards which all the best in me was straining. . . . I had imposed silence on my servant. He died soon after. What I endured after that cannot be described.

ARVIRAGUS: Had you no friend—— ?

JOSEPH: Not one ! Jerusalem was split into rival camps. My old friends were among the unbelievers, my new friends had become the apostles of the " good news," and were united in a joy that kept me always at a distance. I was shut out from both parties—caught in a net that closed ever more tightly about me as the months and years went by. For with their joy in the Resurrection, power had come to the Apostles—power to spread the joy in ever-widening circles. In the end, my one thought was to escape from it all.

ARVIRAGUS: From that power there will be no escape.

JOSEPH: So it seems! I fled from Jerusalem to Damascus, and from Damascus to Antioch. After that I turned westward—passing through one land after another—Syria, Asia, Greece, Macedonia—at every city, before I could settle down, the " good news " had followed me, and the strife in the synagogue would break out, and the party of the Risen Lord—the Christians, as they call themselves—would drive me further afield—further from my native land——

ARVIRAGUS (*softly*): Nearer to Britain. . . .

JOSEPH (*continuing*): A year ago—or was it longer?—I thought I had left them behind me at last for certain. Sailing from Rome, I reached the port of Massilia in Gaul. There is no synagogue in those parts. But this time the Christians had arrived before me. I recognized Philip, one of the oldest disciples, on the quayside.

ARVIRAGUS: And so you sailed again?

JOSEPH: By the first ship that would take me beyond the Pillars of Hercules, out of the Great Sea. . . . The further away the better, I said! I paid the captain well, and—here I am! But the " good news " will pursue me even to Britain, you'll see!

ARVIRAGUS: Others may come after, but you are the first to bring that news to us.

JOSEPH (*miserably*): Only to poison it for you! You know now that the Christ could not have risen!

ARVIRAGUS: Have I not told you that I myself saw him?

JOSEPH: In a vision, perhaps.

ARVIRAGUS: How else except by vision can one see?

JOSEPH: But—with the body still lying in that grave——!

ARVIRAGUS: The body! What is a body—once the spirit has left it? Do you value the chrysalis after the butterfly has flown free?

JOSEPH (*rising, wonder-eyed*): You mean, there can be life—for the earthborn—apart from the body?

ARVIRAGUS: It has been known among us of the Druid cult for generations.

[JOSEPH *breathes a deep sigh of release, then, with his whole body swaying, is seen to be praying silently.* SULI *comes running in from the right.*

SULI: Who's that calling?

[CORDEL'S *voise is heard calling,* " Bran," *as she approaches from the other side.*

It's Mother! (*Calling.*) What is it, Mummy?

133

CORDEL (*off*) : Bran ! Bran ! (*She arrives out of breath.*) Has anybody found him ?

SULI : Is he lost ?

MATUNA : Are you sure he came back ?

CORDEL : Must have come. His boat is in the shed.

ARVIRAGUS : And has he not been seen ?

CORDEL : There was only Camul to question—you know what he is.

SULI : Couldn't you make him understand, Mummy ?

CORDEL : I kept asking him if he'd seen Bran. He just went on mumbling to himself—or rather mumbling to a staff stuck in the ground—*your* staff, I suppose (*to* JOSEPH, *who isn't listening*)— all I could catch was something about a flowering. . . .

SULI : If his boat is in, he must be somewhere on the island.

CORDEL (*dropping suddenly on to a stool*) : I can't move another step.

MATUNA (*going to her*) : No wonder, you poor thing—after these nights of agony——

CORDEL : I didn't want to let him go this morning. He'd been brooding all night. It isn't like Bran to be secretive. We oughtn't to have spoken so freely before him. One forgets he's only a boy. (*Her voice rising shrilly.*) If he's to be taken from me as well as—— It's too much ! I shall—I shall——

ARVIRAGUS (*swiftly at her side*) : Give me your right hand, Cordel. (*Clasping it.*) Now send your mind above that thought.

CORDEL (*struggling with herself*) : I can't ! I can't !

SULI (*desperately*) : Joseph ! (*Appealing to him.*) Aren't you going to help us ?

JOSEPH (*concluding his prayer, takes a deep breath, then suddenly turning to* SULI) : Did you speak to me, my dear ?

SULI : Yes. I asked you to help us.

JOSEPH : Will you first help me—to remove my pack ? (*With her aid, he lowers it carefully to the ground.*) Now at last I am free ! (*To* SULI.) Now—if you will tell me what I am to do——

SULI (*on the verge of tears*) : Bring my brother back.

JOSEPH : That ? (*Taking in the situation.*) I see. (*Power seems to come to him.*) Do not fear. Your brother is safe. (*As though dismissing her, he turns to* ARVIRAGUS.) Sir, I have carried with me from Jerusalem an object of great value which, as I hope to end my days here, I wish to deliver into safe hands.

[*From his knapsack he produces a thickly bound package which he proceeds reverently to unwrap.*

After—after the spirit of Jesus had risen, his mother came to my house to thank me for what I had done. (*He bows his head for some moments.*) She gave me this as a memorial. (*He holds up a small goblet of simple design.*) It was the cup from which he drank on his last night.

[*He hands it to* ARVIRAGUS, *who receives it with equal reverence. The others, sensing a mystery, watch tensely.* CORDEL *has risen to her feet.*

MATUNA (*after a pause*) : May I hold it ?

[JOSEPH *assenting,* ARVIRAGUS *passes the cup to her. She clasps it to her breast, then falls on her knees. Rising again, she meets* CORDEL'S *eye, and turns to* JOSEPH.

May the comfort be shared ? (JOSEPH *raises his hand. Handing the cup to* CORDEL.) He lived for others, and died on a cross.

CORDEL : Come here, Suli. (SULI *goes to her.*) Put your hand with mine. (*They hold it together.*) Somehow I don't feel anxious any more. . . . (*She returns the cup to* MATUNA.)

SULI (*childlike*) : Where are we going to keep it ?

ARVIRAGUS : I will tell you. (*He crosses over to the well and addresses* JOSEPH.) There is a recess concealed within this well which served in ancient times for the performance of rites now no longer practised by us. It has been our custom on certain days to empty the well for purification, and to re-fill it after the sun has set. Old rites and customs must give place to new. But for your coming, I would presently have released the sluice which holds the water from flowing back into the well-chamber. I now propose instead that this cup shall be deposited on the ledge of the recess and that the well shall in future be kept dry for its preservation. Do you approve ? (JOSEPH *inclines his head.*) You can see the ledge from here if you will bend over.

JOSEPH (*obeying, then starting back*) : There is someone standing on the ledge.

[*Exclamations of " What " and " Impossible."*

It is the body of a man.

CORDEL (*her hand to her heart*) : O God !

JOSEPH (*still peering down the well*) : He stirs. He is alive.

ARVIRAGUS : Let me come. (JOSEPH *gives place to him.*)

SULI : Perhaps it's a Roman spy.

ARVIARGUS (*leaning over*) : It is Bran, I think.

135

CORDEL (*running forward*): Bran ! My darling ! (*Kneeling beside* ARVIRAGUS *and calling down the well.*) Bran ! It's your mother. Are you all right ?

BRAN (*crying in reply*): Let me be. *Please*, Mum.

CORDEL (*recoiling*): *Bran !* How came you—— ?

BRAN (*as before*): Of my own free will.

CORDEL: Oh, my son ! The water would have risen and drowned you.

BRAN: I want it to. Let me be. It is my own free will.

ARVIRAGUS (*in a loud voice*): God wills otherwise, my boy ! (*Sternly.*) I order you to return to us. Give me your hand instantly. (*He has stretched forward : his hand is grasped from within.*) Now, spring ! Here ! (BRAN's *free hand seizes hold of the rim of the well.*) And now, forward ! (*He hauls him out, a sturdy lad of fifteen, in loose tunic and close-fitting trousers.*)

CORDEL: Bran ! Oh, Bran ! (*She embraces him.*) Whatever made you do it ?

BRAN (*in tears*): I didn't want to live. I wanted—I wanted——

SULI: I know what he wanted. It was to sacrifice—like in the old days.

ARVIRAGUS (*for* JOSEPH's *benefit*): They have heard from me how, formerly, in times of need, a life, voluntarily dedicated, would be offered to God on behalf of the whole people. (*To* BRAN.) Could you not have spoken to me first ?

MATUNA: Perhaps he wanted to make it easier for us.

BRAN: Wasn't it the right way, Grandpa ?

ARVIRAGUS: It was the old way.

SULI: But you said the new way was all wrong—that no one ought to be sacrificed against his will.

ARVIRAGUS: Yes, that has been our wrong new way.

BRAN: Isn't there any right way, then ?

ARVIRAGUS (*indicating* JOSEPH): One who has come to us from afar will answer.

JOSEPH (*coming forward*): There is an answer in the concluding prayer of our Atonement service : " For I have no pleasure in the death of him that dieth, saith the Lord God ; wherefore turn yourselves and live."

CORDEL (*between her children*): Live ? Perhaps the Romans won't give us a chance !

BRAN: Perhaps they will, Mother, if the rumours on the mainland are true. They say the eastern tribes have risen under Queen Boadicea.

MATUNA (*amid murmurs of relief*): That may mean peace for us in Avalon.

BRAN (*innocently*): What time's supper, Mum ? (CORDEL *looks to* MATUNA.)

MATUNA (*smiling*): Not till sundown, I'm afraid.

SULI: Couldn't he have an apple to go on with ?

MATUNA: The poor boy's hungry ! Of course, Suli. You have one too, dear.

SULI (*losing no time*): Catch, Bran ! (*She throws him an apple from her basket, and they are both munching heartily through the succeeding speeches.*)

MATUNA (*to* JOSEPH): You won't expect a banquet, I hope. There will be bread enough.

ARVIRAGUS: There will be wine for the occasion.

JOSEPH: Bread and wine. Of these he made that last supper, and enriched our table-rites, for remembrance.

ARVIRAGUS: Will you teach us those rites ?

JOSEPH: With his very words.

MATUNA (*still holding the cup*): For the occasion, may this be set before us on the table ?

JOSEPH (*as he nods*): To remember him—only to remember—always . . . if it were possible ! So one might reach to God and make of every day our Day of Atonement.

ARVIRAGUS: Will you teach us also to pray as Israel prays—as he prayed ?

JOSEPH: You have no house for worship ?

ARVIRAGUS: Why should not we build one together ? If our young people will lend a hand——

BRAN (*eagerly*): I know the very place—with plenty of timber handy.

SULI: Please may I make the walls ! I love twining wattles. (*Without waiting for an answer.*) Oh, look ! The sun is setting ! (*She jumps to her feet,* BRAN *following suit. It has begun to darken.*)

MATUNA (to JOSEPH): Will you enter with me? Come, all!

[*Still holding the sangreal, she leads* JOSEPH *into the house.* CORDEL *following with her children on either side.* ARVIRAGUS *remains in meditation for a moment before ending the procession.*

CURTAIN

NOTE AND APOLOGY

" Holyest Erth " was written after a visit in September, 1943, to Chalice Orchard Guest-House* on the slopes of Glastonbury Tor, immediately over-looking the well which provided my setting. The military scene, within the framework of which the action is presented, belongs to authentic Roman-British history, synchronizing nearly enough with the date (A.D. 63) ascribed by William of Malmesbury to the landing of Joseph of Arimathea as the earliest Christian missionary to Britain. The rest is local legend, and presumption—in both senses, perhaps—though at least I did not originate the theory on which Joseph's story of what " really happened " to account for the empty tomb is based. I derived it from Klausner's *Jesus of Nazareth*, and despite the impressive arguments mustered against it in Frank Morison's *Who moved the Stone?* I can still accept it, while owning that I have never been able to believe that the physical body of Jesus rose on the third day, as protested—rather too much, it seems to me—in the Gospels. I want to make it clear that the theory was not adopted by me for dramatic effect. While I have tried to make a good job of the play, nothing is here " for art's sake," and as this is the last (in order of writing) of a series of related pieces, I will take the opportunity of apologizing for much clumsy handling of divine material and at the same time of confiding to any interested reader that one (the secondary) of the two objectives at which I have throughout been aiming is to discover, by experimenting in what I will call the dialogue of auto-psychoanalysis, whether I am a Christian as well as a Jew. Some will find in the heresy of this play a conclusive answer in the negative. Perhaps the Body of the Christ I believe in is more hospitable. I have never felt any more at home in the Church which imposes baptism and a man-made creed on its members than I feel in the Synagogue that demands circumcision (and ignores the New Testament), though I am prepared to believe that the fault, as well as the loss, is mine; it may be " cussedness " rather than heresy that keeps me in " no-man's-land." But I suspect that, sensing deeply the basis of an ultimate reunion of Jew and Christian, I shall go on asking my question, in my own fashion, for my own information while I remain on earth; and I fancy that, so long as I never tire of the subject, while continuing to receive the inestimable blessing of a working faith, I shall, somehow, mysteriously, have plenty to be grateful for.

H. F. R.

* The Guest-House is the property of my friend, Dion Fortune, author of a remarkable book, *The Mystical Qabalah*. The well, which I carefully inspected, forms part of an adjacent property, whose owner will, I hope, forgive me for trespassing.

ALL THINGS ARE POSSIBLE

CHARACTERS

PRISCILLA ⎫ The companions of Paul
AQUILA ⎭

EUNICE   THEODORE   RUFUS ⎫
VERGILIUS   ARISTOBOLUS   MIRIAM ⎬ Christians
FLAVIA   RHODA   JAMES ⎭

JULIAN, husband of Flavia
CORNELIUS, a favourite of the Emperor Nero
MARK, author of the Second Gospel

Scene: A room in the house of Priscilla and Aquila, Rome
Time: A late afternoon in June, A.D. 68

In the back wall is a window, looking on to the street; on the spectators right, towards the front, a door. The furniture has been arranged for what we would call a " drawing-room meeting." Facing the angle between the door-side and the back wall, a table set to accommodate a chairman and a reader. Two rows, formed from a couch and some miscellaneous chairs and stools incline slightly inwards from the door towards the window, leaving clear spaces on all sides. On the near side of the door, a single chair, in isolation.

The style is plain, without suggesting poverty or discomfort.

PRISCILLA, *an elderly woman, tense and bright-eyed, is reclining on the couch, her tablets in her hand, meditating.*

AQUILA, *her husband, enters abruptly, looking for her. He is in a state of suppressed agitation, which emphasizes his Jewish appearance.*

AQUILA: Priscilla !

PRISCILLA (*starting up*) : What is it, my beloved ? (*He drops into the nearest chair, unnerved.*) Aquila ! (*She goes to him.*)

AQUILA: I'm all right now (*Below his breath.*) God give me strength.

PRISCILLA (*quietly*) : Tell me the worst.

AQUILA: Mark—Mark himself——

PRISCILLA: They've taken him ?

AQUILA: I fear so.

PRISCILLA (*nerving herself*) : There is nothing to fear.

AQUILA: I know. I know . . . (*More composed.*) I was just leaving him. One of the women rushed in to warn us. Guardsmen—we could hear their voices. I escaped from the window. With this. (*He draws a cylindrical case from the folds of his toga.*)

PRISCILLA: The new roll ? (*He nods.*) And the other copies——— ?

AQUILA: Already distributed, thank God.

PRISCILLA: Mark remained behind ?

AQUILA: Yes. He said it would be better for all of us.

PRISCILLA: With his Gospel unfinished !

AQUILA: He said if he were meant to finish it, no power could stay him. I never saw him more perfectly controlled.

PRISCILLA (*sitting beside him*): If it had been anyone but Mark !

AQUILA: Remember how we felt when Paul was taken—and all the elders afterwards. The movement goes on. We have only to remain faithful.

PRISCILLA: To-night's meeting—what are we to do about it ?

AQUILA: Mark said we were on no account to put it off. . . . Let me remember his exact directions: he wished nothing to be said that would in any way interfere with the work of the group. I am to announce that he will probably not be with us to-night.

PRISCILLA: " Probably " !

AQUILA: Those were his last words to me. (*He rises and, crossing the room, lays the cylinder on the table.*)

PRISCILLA (*staring before her*): So it begins afresh after a mere respite. . . . How quietly the years have slipped by since that mad blood-bath . . . almost as though Rome had become reconciled to us. . . .

AQUILA (*returning to her*): Would that have been for our good, Priscilla ?

PRISCILLA: You are right. To find security in the world of to-day —a world ruled by Nero ! (*She shudders.*) God forbid !

AQUILA: Such a world ! How one nightmare succeeds another ! They were gossiping in the Forum this morning of yet another crisis. The whole Western Army is now said to be in revolt. Perhaps—who knows ?—we are to be blamed for that, as, last time, for the firing of Rome !

PRISCILLA: Someone is coming. . . . (*Rising.*) My tablets ! (*She retrieves them from the couch, as a gentle treble knock at the door is followed by the entry of a young couple,* EUNICE *and* VERGILIUS.)

EUNICE (*looking round*): Are we the first again?

PRISCILLA (*recording their names, with a stylus, on the waxen tablet*): Eunice, Vergilius. . . . (*Looking up with a smile.*) Someone has to be first, Eunice. (*She has stationed herself in the chair by the door.* AQUILA *remains standing.*)

EUNICE: The time always seems to drag so before a meeting!

VERGILIUS (*seating himself in the front row*): I hear James may be coming to-night.

AQUILA: If he arrives in time, and is not too exhausted.

EUNICE: As well the poor man may be after travelling in this heat! (*She has taken a seat beside* VERGILIUS.) I've never known the city more stifling!

[*The three knocks, as before, and* FLAVIA *enters. She is a woman, in the late thirties, of a delicate beauty.*

PRISCILLA (*noting her name*): Flavia.

FLAVIA (*looking round, anxiously*): I was hoping Mark would be here. . . .

AQUILA: Is anything the matter? (*He is still standing by the table.*)

FLAVIA: My husband is waiting for me outside. I want to ask permission to bring him in. . . .

AQUILA (*surprised*): Your husband? But he is not a church-member.

FLAVIA (*nervously*): That was what I was going to explain——

[*Another treble knock, and three people enter together.* THEODORE *and* ARISTOBOLUS, *young men of earnest and studious appearance, and* RHODA, *a tight-lipped spinster of* FLAVIA'S *generation.*

PRISCILLA (*taking their names*): Theodore, Aristobolus. (*They go quietly to stools.*) Rhoda. . . .

RHODA (*lingering*): Mother won't be coming to-night.

[PRISCILLA *nods, and she proceeds to take her seat.* AQUILA, *meanwhile, has seated himself at the table.*

AQUILA: Our sister Flavia was broaching a personal matter. . . .

FLAVIA: If you could spare me a minute. . . . It means such a lot to me. . . . (AQUILA *nods assent.*) I want to bring my husband to the meeting. I know it must sound very unusual. I wouldn't ask if I hadn't a special reason. . . . (*With emotion.*) Ever since I joined the church, my hope and prayer has been to win him over to us. It's been so hateful having something I couldn't share with him. Perhaps I was over-anxious. . . .

[She is interrupted by a further knocking, heralding the entrance of RUFUS, *a middle-aged Roman of dignified bearing, and* MIRIAM, *a nervous young Jewess, his wife.*

PRISCILLA (*murmuring as she writes*): Rufus, Miriam. . . .

AQUILA (*as they tiptoe to their places*): Yes, Flavia?

FLAVIA: May I go straight on? I'll be as brief as possible. . . . I took my husband to a church service soon after my conversion. I can see now that it was a mistake to try that way. He's a very fastidious man. He was just repelled by the untrained singing, and the smells of the slaves, and by what he called "crude emotionalism" . . .

[Again a knocking, and JAMES, *a grizzled veteran of patriarchal features, joins the gathering.*

PRISCILLA (*unable to restrain a special note of welcome*): James!

JAMES (*noticing* FLAVIA's *preoccupation*): Ssh! (*He slips into the nearest seat.*)

AQUILA (*to* FLAVIA): The service didn't appeal to him, you say?

FLAVIA: No, and that made it so difficult. Then this study circle was formed, and I saw my chance. Gradually he's been growing less critical. Other things have helped. Business worries and changes in our circumstances have taught him, I think, to take life more seriously. I needn't go into all that. . . . To my great joy, as I was starting out this afternoon, he told me he'd had a vision. Then he asked, quite humbly, if he might come with me. . . . I'm so anxious not to miss the opportunity. As I say, he's waiting outside here now.

[A pause.

AQUILA (*doubtfully*): It is our sister's husband, James. . . .

JAMES: Will Mark not be coming this evening?

AQUILA: I should have mentioned that before. He asked me to say he would probably be prevented. . . .

PRISCILLA: I've had messages from everyone else, I think. (*Referring to her list.*) Yes, we are all present.

AQUILA: Does anybody wish to express an opinion?

RHODA (*after some hesitation*): The rule is surely quite clear? Whoever wants to bring a stranger to our meetings has to give at least one week's notice. Moreover, the candidate must already be a member of the church.

FLAVIA: My husband could hardly be regarded as a stranger. The Apostle Paul himself laid it down——

RHODA: Pardon, sister, but we are discussing the rules of a private group formed more than a year after Paul's death.

ARISTOBOLUS: I agree with our sister Flavia that for general purposes the husband or wife of a member is to be distinguished from an ordinary stranger. Indeed, our rule of secrecy expressly recognizes the overriding privileges of the marriage tie. But I for one was not aware of any similar qualification of the rule governing new membership.

FLAVIA (*desperately*): Are not exceptions admitted to every rule, in special cases? I'm putting this forward as a special case.

AQUILA: I think our sister is entitled to do that.

VERGILIUS: May I ask if anyone here is acquainted with the candidate?

FLAVIA: Mark knows him . . . slightly.

RHODA: I know him well. (*She pauses.*) I am sorry that I must offend our sister's feelings. I am emphatically against admitting him.

FLAVIA: May I ask why?

RHODA: Since you press me, I think he is not to be trusted.

FLAVIA: And you say you know him!

RHODA: I have known him since he was a boy.

FLAVIA (*almost in tears*): You are prejudiced against him!

AQUILA (*too mildly protesting*): Sisters, sisters!

RHODA: I am not in the least prejudiced. I give it as my honest opinion that your husband is a thoroughly unprincipled man.

FLAVIA (*wildly*): You have never forgiven him for marrying me! (*She bursts into tears.*)

JAMES (*in his deep voice*): May I ask for silence? (*A pause.*) Beloved, if we look into ourselves, which of us must not feel humiliated by this outburst? Consider, we put bits in horses' mouths so that they may obey us, and we may turn about their whole bodies. If we could but bridle our own bodies! The tongue is such a little member, yet not one of us can tame it. And see what mischief it works! It is like fire——

FLAVIA (*in a low voice*): I am ashamed. I ask our sister's forgiveness.

RHODA (*jerkily*): It is for me to ask forgiveness. You were quite right. I was jealous when Julian preferred you to me. I have never conquered my jealousy. I have no right to judge him. I withdraw my objection. . . .

AQUILA (*gravely*): There remains the important question of principle. In the absence of Mark, I think we ought to ask ourselves what may have been the real object of the rule we are discussing. Surely it was to enable the fullest enquiries to be made regarding the suitability of a candidate?

THEODORE: From the point of view of right understanding?

AQUILA: From every point of view.

THEODORE: You mean, it was primarily a precaution against informers?

EUNICE: Imposed at a time when they were known to be active! At least, we can dismiss *that* consideration from our minds.

[PRISCILLA, *about to interpose, catches* AQUILA'S *eye and checks herself.*

FLAVIA: Brethren, forgive me if I seem importunate. To me, the case is so simple. My husband's love is at stake. Since this barrier came between us, it has been such misery. And now—now that, after all my efforts, there seems a real hope of removing it——

PRISCILLA: If the hope is well-founded, Flavia, a week's delay could surely do no harm?

FLAVIA: Oh, Priscilla, are *you* against me?

THEODORE: Priscilla's argument cuts both ways, I think. If the hope should prove illusory, what harm could be done by testing it now?

JAMES (*unexpectedly*): I am for granting our sister's request.

[*Other voices:* " And I."

PRISCILLA: It is the feeling of the majority, I see.

AQUILA (*to* FLAVIA): Will your husband understand our procedure?

FLAVIA: I can easily explain it to him. He's very quick-minded. . . . I'll go at once, if I may. Oh, thank you. . . .

[*She hurries out. There is a pause.*

RUFUS: Beloved, I should have spoken before, perhaps; I could not make up my mind. I have a suspicion against this man, our sister's husband.

MIRIAM (*with a slight cry*): Rufus!

RUFUS: A suspicion. No more. I know him by sight only. I chanced to see him recently conferring with a certain colleague of mine at the Ministry—a notorious Palace creature. It crossed my mind that they were planning mischief. I trust I was mistaken.

PRISCILLA: I think we ought to face the possibility that Rufus was not mistaken——

MIRIAM (*excitedly*): There have been such terrible rumours about the Emperor lately. They were saying yesterday——

PRISCILLA: Please, Miriam ! Let us all keep our heads. Suppose the worst: suppose that our lives are in the hands of this man, a man capable of betraying his own wife——

THEODORE: If we were to disperse at once——

VERGILIUS: We should stand self-condemned.

ARISTOBOLUS: Our lives don't matter so much. It's Mark's Gospel that matters. If some parchment were to fall into his hands——

AQUILA: Other copies would remain, already transmitted to specially appointed custodians; our secretarial groups have seen to that. . . . James, what do you counsel ?

JAMES: I see only one danger: the fear of man. I know only one way to avoid it : it is the way which we meet here of purpose to study. Is there any reason why we should not proceed with our meeting ?

AQUILA: And—you mean ?—receive this man——

JAMES: As our sister Flavia would expect us to receive him.

PRISCILLA: I agree with James.

AQUILA: Does anyone dissent ? (*No answer.*) I propose, then, that we commence as usual by directing our minds to last week's reading. (*A pause of concentration.*) Are there any questions ?

EUNICE: There was a passage about the Mosaic law of divorce which didn't seem clear to a non-Jewish listener.

AQUILA: Can you remember the context ?

EUNICE: It was leading up to a saying about the marriage state . . .

AQUILA: What was the saying ? (*A treble knock at the door, and* FLAVIA *returns with* JULIAN, *her husband. The latter, an attractive and vital personality, bows a little over-deferentially to* AQUILA, *who courteously motions him to be seated. The rest remain rigidly attentive.* FLAVIA *leads* JULIAN *to a vacant place at the front end of the first row, before returning to her former seat. Meanwhile*) Yes, sister Eunice ?

EUNICE: It was said that God made man and woman, and ordained that a man should break away from his family to unite himself with a wife.

AQUILA: And after that ?

EUNICE: It concluded: those whom God has joined, let not man put asunder.

AQUILA: Correct. Do you think an exposition of the Mosaic law of divorce would make the matter any clearer?

EUNICE (*after a pause*): No. I hadn't thought rightly about it.

AQUILA: Are there any other questions? (*No response. He addresses* JULIAN.) As you are no doubt aware, brother, we are occupied at these meetings with a narrative, not yet completed, of things said and things done by our master, Jesus of Nazareth.

JULIAN: Him you call the Christ?

AQUILA: Yes. It is compiled from notes, recording conversations, extending over many years, with one who was closely associated with Jesus. We read new portions as they come to us from the author week by week.

JULIAN: The author is a certain Marcus, I believe.

AQUILA (*proceeding, after a slight pause*): Many of the sayings are difficult to understand. We have been told that, to grasp the inner meaning, it is necessary that our minds should be like those of little children.

JULIAN: You allow questions, do you not?

AQUILA: We invite them.

JULIAN: Thank you.

AQUILA: The portion we were reading last week described how Jesus taught in the temple of Jerusalem, while his enemies were devising plots against him. We have here a continuation. . . . (*He opens the cylindrical box, extracts from it a scroll of parchment, which he lays on the table, placing the empty box on the floor.*) Vergilius?

[VERGILIUS *comes forward, seats himself at the table beside him, takes the scroll and proceeds to read slowly and distinctly.*

VERGILIUS: " They sent certain Legalists and Herodians to catch him in his words. They came up to him and said: ' Rabbi, we know you are sincere and outspoken; you do not toady to the authorities, you teach the true way of God. Is it right that we should pay taxes to the Emperor? Ought we to pay or not to pay?' He saw through their hypocrisy, and said: 'Why do you seek to trap me? Bring me a penny. Let me look at it.' They brought him one. He said: ' Whose likeness and whose inscription is this?' They said: ' Cæsar's.' Jesus answered: ' Render to Cæsar the things that are Cæsar's, and to God the things that are God's.' They were abashed." (*He pauses.*)

JULIAN: As well they might be ! And that, I take it, represents the official attitude of the sect towards any holder of the Imperial office?

FLAVIA (*aghast*): Julian !

JULIAN: I beg your pardon. I understood we were entitled to ask questions ?

AQUILA (*unruffled*): We usually reserve our questions until the conclusion of the reading.

JULIAN: I see. I must apologize.

AQUILA: Will you continue, Vergilius ?

VERGILIUS (*as before*): " Presently a scribe, who had been listening carefully, and was impressed by the aptness of his answers, came forward and asked: ' Which is the greatest of all the commandments ? ' Jesus answered: ' The greatest commandemnt is " Hear, O Israel, the Lord our God is one. Love the Lord your God with your whole heart, your whole soul, your whole mind, and your whole strength." And after that commandment, " Love your neighbour as yourself." No other commandments are as great as these.' The scribe said: ' Master, that is the truth. There is one God, and none other than He. And to love him with our whole heart, our whole understanding, our whole strength, and to love our neighbour as ourself, is worth more than all the burnt offerings and sacrifices.' Jesus saw that he understood, and said: ' You are not far from the kingdom of God.' . . . After that, no one ventured to put any more questions to him."

AQUILA: Will you pause there, Vergilius. . . .

JULIAN (*with unconcealed mockery*): May I now put my question ?

 [FLAVIA *gasps*.

AQUILA (*with a slight pause*): Before you do so, as you are a newcomer, it would be as well, I think, for me to explain——

JULIAN (*with a smile*): That inconvenient questions are barred, perhaps ?

FLAVIA: Julian ! Julian !

AQUILA (*more sternly*): Only one kind of question is ruled out by us: the dishonest kind. . . . (*Quietly impressive.*) This is what I want to say. We are a group of people united by a single aim: the fulfilment of a common spiritual need. You have come here by your own wish. You are free to remain. But if you do so, we shall expect you to abide by our rules. Our first rule is absolute frankness. Working as a group, we know that our aim can be served only by—as it were—pooling the knowledge of which every one of us possesses some fragment. It is a mutual obligation. If you decide to remain among us, we shall conceal nothing from you, and we shall require you to conceal nothing from us. Is that clear ?

JULIAN: You want me to take some form of oath, I suppose?

AQUILA: Nothing of the kind. . . . But I think we should all of us like to have some assurance from you as to your motive in coming here. (*Murmurs of approval.*)

FLAVIA (*as* JULIAN *hesitates*): May I speak for him? (*Looking straight at him.*) He was directed by a vision: an angel signed to him to follow his wife. . . . Or was that not the truth, Julian?

JULIAN (*as steadily*): It was a bare-faced lie, my dear.

FLAVIA: Ah! You admit it? Then will you explain——? (*Suddenly averting her face.*) No, no. Don't tell me! I couldn't bear to hear it. . . .

JULIAN (*coolly*): I propose to enlighten you, none the less. (*Turning to* AQUILA.) You shall see, all of you, that I am not afraid to speak the truth. Nay, I can go further with you. You tell me it is a spiritual need that brings you together. Well, it is a spiritual need —as I understand the term—that has drawn me into this charmed circle. So, by your leave, I will remain here and give you frankness for frankness.

AQUILA: By all means. Do you still wish to ask a question about our attitude towards the Emperor?

FLAVIA (*interposing*): *I* have a question to ask—an urgent question. . . . About loving. (*She pauses, overcome with emotion.*)

AQUILA: Yes, sister?

FLAVIA: I have tried my hardest to fulfil the commandment—to love God and to love my neighbour. Perhaps I'm not big enough. Perhaps I just didn't understand. . . . To love God, as I saw it, was to love good—to love good wherever one saw good. I saw my husband as good. My husband was also my neighbour. It was so easy to love my husband, so much easier than to love God. I believed God loved me, but I *knew* my husband loved me. I had his own word for it. And now—now I know that my husband's word was a lie, and that what I took for good was bad. And all my love has gone—my love for God as well as for my neighbour. . . . How am I to go on living? (*She breaks down completely.*)

JULIAN (*ironically*): What has the learned oracle to say to that poser?

AQUILA (*addressing* FLAVIA): Our brother James has often spoken of the value of these setbacks and trials as tests of faith. . . .

FLAVIA: I have no faith. My faith has been destroyed. . . .

JAMES: So you think. This happens to all of us at times. You must be patient.

PRISCILLA: We know the agony you are going through, sister. We know that it passes.

THEODORE: We are here to help you.

FLAVIA (*roused*): No, no, that is impossible. (*She rises unsteadily.*) All the meaning has gone—it could never be the same again. . . . (*She moves towards the door.*)

JULIAN (*following her*): Where are you going, Flavia?

FLAVIA (*dully*): Does it matter?

JAMES (*loudly*): Your faith will return, sister.

JULIAN (*turning to him*): Never, I say! Never! . . . (*Drawing himself up.*) And she has a husband's love to thank for it!

FLAVIA (*arrested*): Love—love, did you say?

JULIAN: A husband's love! (*She stares at him.*) Yes, you can look at me. I am no mythical theological abstraction, but flesh and blood, a human being, a reality.

FLAVIA (*incredulous*): You say you love me?

JULIAN: Yes, it is time your eyes were opened. You have been deceived in many things—never in my love for you. For my own confessed deception—the stratagem by means of which I obtained this introduction to your interesting Jewish friends—I make no apology. Your case was desperate: desperate measures were called for, and they have been successful. Already you are cured of your obsession—this so-called faith in a God that has never existed outside the distorted Oriental imagination. You thought you loved him—this moonshine deity—as you loved me, your husband. Nay, you loved him before me, and so made me jealous of my rival. . . . He is no more. The spell is broken. My love remains. Build on it, if you will, a new faith—faith in life! It will prove a sure foundation.

[*A gesture from* AQUILA *checks some muttering among the seated Christians.*

FLAVIA (*faintly*): Was it for . . . no more than this . . . that you deceived me?

JULIAN: It must all seem strange to you at first, I know. (*Suddenly she reels. He goes to support her.*) You have had a great shock.

FLAVIA: Yes. (*She frees herself.*) I feel better now. You have removed a fear . . .

JULIAN (*gently*): You must go home and lie down—rest yourself, body and mind . . .

FLAVIA: Yes . . . (*As she turns away, further murmurs are again silenced by* AQUILA. *She pauses.*) Are you not coming with me?

JULIAN: Not yet, my love.

FLAVIA (*terror returning*): Why not?

JULIAN: I have business to transact.

[*Signs of frayed nerves are again manifest among the attentive listeners.*

FLAVIA: Business? Here?

JULIAN: You shall learn all in good time.

FLAVIA: What are you concealing from me? You told me you had accomplished your object in coming here? (*As he hesitates.*) You promised to be frank?

JULIAN: Very well. . . . I had a two-fold object. It is the main object I have accomplished.

FLAVIA: And the other?

JULIAN: I have undertaken to obtain material for a report.

[*A slight gasping betrays the weaker members of the group.*

FLAVIA (*recoiling*): What kind of a report?

JULIAN: Since you insist on knowing . . . (*his confidence returning*) a report which I have reason to believe will be of some interest to the Emperor. (*A cry of horror escapes her.* AQUILA's *restraining hand steadies the others.* JULIAN *proceeds ruthlessly.*) His Majesty seeks information as to whether a certain obscure cult has survived the measures taken to exterminate it after the great fire.

FLAVIA: My fear—my fear——

JAMES (*with the voice of authority*): What man is to be feared? Only God has strength.

JULIAN: What man is to be feared? Well said, Rabbi! (*Looking around.*) Have I been frank enough for you so far? Have I not scrupulously respected your rules?

FLAVIA (*covering her face*): What have I done?

JULIAN (*challengingly*): What are you going to do now? I am entirely in the hands of the meeting!

[*A pause. Then some renewed murmuring.*

MIRIAM (*audibly*): We could overpower him easily.

[*One or two of the men half-rise in response.*

JAMES (*peremptorily*): No.

AQUILA: Let everyone remain seated.

[*Discipline is reasserted. During the succeeding speeches a strained stillness prevails.*

JULIAN: As I expected. (*Turning to* FLAVIA.) Fear nobody and nothing. Only trust me. I am no fool. I know quite well what I'm about. It was an inspiration!

FLAVIA (*as one groping in the dark*): You spoke just now of loving me still . . . ?

JULIAN: What I now do is proof. Cæsar's reward for my services: a love-token !

FLAVIA (*revolted*): Money !

JULIAN: Do you despise money ? Your new faith will teach you better ! Have patience ! You shall see how accurately I have diagnosed your case, how this day's work solves all our problems ! Let me tell you what really brought you into this congregation: it was shortage of money, my dear—material discomfort. You sought relief, an escape, from reality: you found it in this superstition of "Christian" comfort ! Your "spiritual need" will in future be satisfied by more normal expedients ! Our troubles are at an end ! Henceforth we are going to live on the fat of the land, bask in the sunshine. . . . It will work real miracles, I promise you ! A month from now, and you will be looking back on this mystical interlude as on some wildly fantastic dream after daylight has woken you. . . . Or do you begin to see daylight already ?

FLAVIA: I am trying to see—I want to see—everything—clearly. . . . This report of yours—what will come of it ? For you, advancement—I see that. But for these—my friends—— ?

JULIAN: That will be for the Emperor to decide. . . . You will not miss them. Friends ! You will have all the friends you want, from the cream of Court circles. . . .

FLAVIA: They are to be sacrificed, for your—our—benefit ?

JULIAN: The weak must go down before the strong. It is the way of life.

FLAVIA: It is the way of life. Yes, I see that quite clearly.

[*A sudden renewed stir among the members of the group momentarily diverts attention.* MIRIAM *is clinging to her husband.*

MIRIAM (*in gasps*): It's all right. I know they can't really part us. Just take no notice of me. Please. . . .

[*She gradually relaxes, and the stillness returns.*

JULIAN (*with a shrug*): They are to be pitied, perhaps. I know your tender heart. Were they not strangers to me, even I might commiserate.

FLAVIA: Strangers . . . strangers . . .

JULIAN: Unless, by chance—— (*He turns to examine his prospective victims.*) Why, if it isn't Rhoda, of all unlikely people! Rhoda, the gay, irrepressible, daredevil—— !

153

RHODA (*gently*) : Yes, Julian.

JULIAN : Flavia, you should have told me ! You must take her home with you.

FLAVIA : You think she would come ?

JULIAN : Surely ? Why—do you remember, Rhoda ?—we used to be quite fond of one another.

RHODA : I think I love you still, Julian. If I could save you——

JULIAN : *You* save *me* ? The rôles are to be reversed, are they ? (*Suspiciously.*) May I ask what you have in mind ?

RHODA : A saying we heard last week. . . . The words have escaped me. It was about a camel.

JULIAN : A camel ! Are you quite mad ?

AQUILA : Can anyone remember the passage ?

EUNICE : " How hard is it for them that trust in riches to enter into the Kingdom of God. It is easier for a camel to go through the eye of a needle."

JULIAN (*laughing*) : So that's all it was !

RHODA : No. There was something after. " The disciples asked, ' Who then can be saved ? ' And he answered : ' With men it is impossible, but not with God, for with God all things are possible.' "

JULIAN (*roughly*) : That's enough. My time is short. Do you reject my offer ? (*She smiles, enraging him.*) You think Nero's methods of punishment a laughing matter ? So be it ! (*He goes to the window, takes a coloured scarf from his gown, and waves it as a signal. Then striding back, he flings open the door, and turns sharply to his wife.*) Now go—quickly.

[*The sudden climax momentarily shakes the control of the group.*

VERGILIUS (*rearing himself, impulsively*) : The outer door—shall I secure it ?

PRISCILLA (*rising in turn, to bar his way*) : There are no fastenings to the doors of our house, Vergilius.

JULIAN (*excitedly*) : Flavia ! Do you hear me ? You must go at once !

FLAVIA : I go to my place. Among the weak.

[*She returns to her former seat, bringing tranquility to the whole group again.*

JULIAN (*staggered*) : What ? But your faith—you said I had destroyed it ?

FLAVIA : That is true.

JULIAN: So, in revenge, you would cut off your nose to spite your face?

FLAVIA (*sadly*): If you could only understand——

JULIAN (*desperately*): Listen to me. You saw me signal from the window: any minute now the responsibility will be taken out of my hands. Do you wish to condemn yourself to a horrible death for a faith which you have declared you no longer hold? Is that what I am to understand?

FLAVIA: I am so sorry for you, Julian.

JULIAN: Sorry—for me? (*Desperately.*) Then go—if not for your own sake, for my sake. I love you. I love you, I say.

FLAVIA: You love so many things, my husband. . . .

JULIAN: What have I done?

[*Enter* CORNELIUS, *a youngish man, foppishly bejewelled and bloated with dissipation.* JULIAN *shrinks from him.*

CORNELIUS: My compliments, Julian. Truly a snug little synagogue! (*Looking round.*) All alive and unresisting, eh? (*Clapping him on the shoulder.*) Cæsar will be enchanted! (*Observing the manuscript on the table.*) And documentary evidence into the bargain! (*He goes to take it.*)

JULIAN (*in a strained voice*): One moment. (CORNELIUS *stops.*) That document is of no significance whatever—a dull historical treatise——

CORNELIUS: What?

JULIAN (*averting his eyes*): I have to ask your pardon. I have made a horrible mistake.

CORNELIUS (*with an ugly look*): What do you say?

JULIAN: I have no evidence against these people. The meeting was not what I expected. It is a harmless literary society. . . .

CORNELIUS: Are you attempting some feeble jest?

JULIAN: I ought to have made more careful inquiries—I realise now——

CORNELIUS: You are serious? (*Quivering with rage.*) You actually have the effrontery—after allowing me, *me*, to make all the arrangements—including the trifling detail of arresting the accused Marcus in his own house——! With Cæsar waiting at this very minute to receive us at the Palace—you coolly announce that you've simply been making a fool of me!

JULIAN: I have no excuse—I accept full responsibility——

155

CORNELIUS (*with a snarl*): Very handsome of you ! By the Gods, you'll pay for this ! Cæsar's appetite has already been whetted. . . . If I know anything of my master, he will not be done out of his entertainment. He is in no merciful mood these days. At least your body will serve his purpose !

JULIAN: I am quite prepared to take all the consequences.

CORNELIUS (*grimly*): We shall see ! (*He moves towards the door,* JULIAN *following.*)

FLAVIA: Julian ! (*As* CORNELIUS *turns.*) I am his wife.

CORNELIUS (*icily*): You have my sympathy.

JULIAN (*taking her aside*): Your God has beaten me, Flavia.

FLAVIA: Oh, my husband !

JULIAN: It's the end, my dear. I haven't a dog's chance.

FLAVIA: Don't say that !

JULIAN: We'll say I have a camel's chance, then. (*He embraces her.*)

CORNELIUS (*sharply*): I thought you were ready.

FLAVIA (*to* CORNELIUS): May I come with him to the Palace ?

CORNELIUS (*with a leer*): I shouldn't advise you to come inside.

FLAVIA: As far as the Palace, then ?

CORNELIUS: You can please yourself about that. (*He stalks out, motioning them to follow.*)

FLAVIA: Come, Julian.

[*She leads him out after* CORNELIUS. PRISCILLA *closes the door. A long silence.*

RHODA (*thinking aloud*): Oh God, be merciful to him !

JAMES: Prayer, rightly used, can help.

PRISCILLA: Mark may be in danger still.

EUNICE: And we didn't know he was arrested even !——

[*The familiar treble knock at the door rouses a sudden tension. All eyes are turned to the door.* MARK, *a lean, deep-eyed, scholarly ascetic, enters briskly.*

AQUILA (*in unrestrained relief*): Mark ! (*He rises with difficulty.*)

MARK (*quietly*): I am sorry to be so late. (*He crosses to take the chair vacated by* AQUILA.) Vergilius has been reading from the new scroll ?

VERGILIUS (*hardly taking in the words*): I—you said—?—I beg your pardon——

156

JAMES: We are all in bewilderment, brother. We heard you had been arrested.

MARK (*displeased*): I had hoped that matter would not be broached. The work of this group is unconnected with external events . . .

AQUILA: Nothing was said by me, brother. (*He is now seated in the body of the meeting.*)

PRISCILLA: Cornelius, the Court parasite, has just left here.

MARK: I see. (*Unbending.*) There was a litter turning the corner as I entered. . . .

PRISCILLA: Nero is awaiting him at the Palace. You were to have been charged before him.

MARK: Yes. . . . Cornelius has left it too late. He will not be well received at the Palace. Nero has fled from Rome.

RHODA (*above general murmurs of joyful thanksgiving*): Then Julian is saved. . . . O God !

MARK (*forestalling any further demonstration*): Has there been no reading at all ?

AQUILA: A start was made. . . .

MARK: Our time is very precious . . . Vergilius, will you continue, please ?

VERGILIUS (*reading as before*): " And as he taught in the Temple, he said to his disciples . . . "

THE CURTAIN IS FALLING

FAREWELL, JERUSALEM

CHARACTERS

RABBI JOHANAN BEN ZAKKAI
MILCAH, his sister
DAVID, his son
BEN BATIAH,* his nephew
JOANNA, a Christian Jewess
JOSHUA BEN HANANIAH, a disciple of the Rabbi
ELIEZER BEN HYRCANUS ⎫
Three other disciples ⎭ in non-speaking parts

Scene: Rabbi Johanan ben Zakkai's house in Jerusalem
Time: April of the year A.D. 69

RABBI JOHANAN'S *house, like the structure of his mind, is solid and devoid of æsthetic appeal. In the principal living-room the furniture is plain and scanty, the curtain-hangings faded. There are three exits; a strong double-panelled bolted door on the spectators' right giving access to the street, a curtained opening in the back of the opposite wall leading into an inner room, and towards the front of the latter wall a substantial hinged panel concealing a stairway to the cellar.*

At the rise of the curtain, the stage is unoccupied. Presently, from the distance, comes the sound of horns stating and repeating an ascending phrase of two or three notes, signalling an alarm, accompanied by the sound of scurrying footsteps in the street. Then there is a quiet tapping at the front door, repeated with gradually increasing force, until MILCAH, *the Rabbi's sister, an elderly woman, hollow-eyed and tense, entering through the curtain, goes to the front door and calls.*

MILCAH (*in a hoarse voice*): Who is it?

A WOMAN'S VOICE (*from without*): Joanna. Reuben's daughter.

[MILCAH *draws back in surprise, then, collecting herself, calls through the curtains to someone within.*

MILCAH: It's no one important. You can leave it to me.

JOANNA: Please let me in!

[*Grudgingly* MILCAH *unbolts and opens the door, admitting a youngish woman, bright-eyed, but quietly controlled. There is an embarrassed silence.*

MILCAH: You can't stay here! I'm sorry.

JOANNA: You heard the blower?

* Pronounced Bateeah.

MILCAH: Yes, the third already to-day ! You'll find shelter in the school-house. It's only a few steps away.

[*Sounds of approaching soldiery become audible.*

JOANNA: I'm afraid there's no time.

MILCAH (*angrily*): Come inside—quickly.

JOANNA: Oh, thank you.

MILCAH (*as she bolts the door behind her*): No woman in her senses would have ventured out on a day like this ! (*Moving away.*) You can sit down, if you like.

JOANNA (*not moving*): I want to see David, please. I came here purposely.

MILCAH (*astonished*): You came here to see David ? (*Abruptly.*) Well, you can't. My nephew has duties to attend to. You have not heard, perhaps—— ?

JOANNA: Of his father's death ? Yes, I heard yesterday. . . . I brought a few flowers for you. (*Delivering them.*)

MILCAH (*touched*): That was kind of you. (*She hesitates for a moment.*) You can't see David to-day. It's out of the question.

[*A body of soldiers passes outside, producing a din of ribald singing and shouting. The two women instinctively draw closer together.*

JOANNA: It's the new lot—from the South—by their voices. I heard they'd been looting the wine-shops.

MILCAH: Yes, like all the rest of them—extremists, counter-extremists, whatever fancy names they may give themselves ! Devils ! Devils one and all !

JOANNA: It's sometimes better when they're drunk.

MILCAH: They say there'll be bloody fighting presently. Both sides have been massing. . . .

JOANNA: Yes. (*A slight pause. The noise diminishes.*) They're passing already.

MILCAH (*mechanically*): Thank God ! (*As the tension relaxes.*) Now we shall have the " All clear " perhaps.

JOANNA: Meanwhile, won't you please let David know I'm here ? I won't keep him long.

MILCAH (*relenting*): Well, I'll just go upstairs and see. . . . (*She sways suddenly.*) No, I must sit down for a moment.

JOANNA (*helping her to a chair*): You have been overtaxing your strength.

MILCAH: I'll be all right if you don't fuss me. Sit down yourself. (JOANNA *obeys.*) How is your mother keeping ? But she died of the plague, didn't she ?

JOANNA: Yes, just before the last insurrection. That awful day, with the rain and the blood pouring down the Lower City——

MILCAH: I should have said I was sorry.

JOANNA: Oh, why? We felt no sorrow—only deep relief that she should have found peace. Don't you feel that way about your bereavement? (MILCAH *tightens her lips.*) There is a difference, I know. The Rabbi, your brother, was a man—and such a man! Strong as a lion in his faith! He was my hero from childhood——

MILCAH (*softly*): Yes, a hero. A great hero of Israel. His name will live.

JOANNA: And yet—how he must have suffered during all these last terrible months . . . and in the last weeks——

MILCAH: You need not speak of them.

JOANNA: No. And now—now, at least, he is safe.

MILCAH (*fiercely*): He was always safe. They could never harm him.

JOANNA: They would have laid hands on him. The net grows tighter every day.

MILCAH (*changing the subject, in a tone of malicious irony*): Things get no better, eh? You have noticed that?

JOANNA (*with a sigh*): There was a time when one used to say, " Well, at least things can't get any worse "—and then, the next day or the day after, would come some shattering new crisis or calamity. . . . Do you remember? All that seems to belong to a remote past. A new abomination nowadays is received almost as a matter of course.

MILCAH: And where is it going to end, do you think? In the overthrowing of the mighty Roman Empire by rival gangs of demented ruffians at present occupied in killing each other off as fast as they can to prove their patriotism? (JOANNA *is silent.*) My question embarrasses you!

JOANNA: Embarrasses? You couldn't think, surely——?

MILCAH (*bitterly*): I think we are living in a Jerusalem where to speak the truth is to risk the death of a traitor—where informers are handsomely rewarded—where one's best friends have been driven desperate by hunger! I think a prudent person will trust no one.

JOANNA (*sadly*): You have trusted me, it seems. (*A series of blasts on a high note, long sustained, is heard from the distant horns.*) Listen! The " All Clear " again!

MILCAH: Yes, all clear—all clear—what could be clearer?

(*Echoing the note of the horn in a quavering voice.*) Jerusalem, thy days are numbered ! (*The tension has snapped, and her pent-up emotions dissolve in a sudden flood of tears.*) Take no notice of me ! (*She cries unrestrainedly.*)

JOANNA (*in a soothing voice*) : As though I could ever feel mistrust or suspicion in this house ! My other home : you commanded me to call it that, you know ! It was on the day you came to take charge, after David's mother died. I couldn't have been more than five.

MILCAH (*steadied*) : David was six. I hoped it would really become your home in those days. . . . Those days ! The days when you used to call me " Auntie."

JOANNA : I still think of you as Auntie. One doesn't forget. (*She glances round the room.*) If you knew how often I have revisited this room—in my thoughts and dreams ! Even the pattern of those old curtains has remained in my memory ! With how much besides ! I remember David showing me the way to the cellar (*she points to the door*), and what fun we used to have down there !

MILCAH : What a fright you gave us that first time !

JOANNA : I thought you were never going to forgive me ! And it really wasn't all my fault.

MILCAH : I have been angrier with you since. Perhaps I won't ever forgive you—for not marrying David. *That* was all your fault.

JOANNA : It was nobody's fault, Auntie.

MILCAH : Did *he* give *you* up ? He is still unmarried, you know.

JOANNA : I, too. . . . But how unimportant all that has become !

MILCAH : Yes, you are right there. To think of marriage under this rule of wild beasts ! . . . All the same, Joanna——

JOANNA : All the same, I haven't changed, Auntie.

MILCAH : You still worship with those people ?

JOANNA : Call us Christians—we've accepted the name, you know. . . . Some things, even in this chaos, remain unchanged and unchangeable.

MILCAH (*sternly*) : Judaism is one.

JOANNA : I am a Jewess still.

MILCAH : A strange Judaism that can be shared with the un-circumcized !

JOANNA : Still Judaism, for me.

MILCAH : Not the Judaism of Jerusalem.

JOANNA : Did you not say yourself, Jerusalem's days are numbered ?

MILCAH: Yes, because she has not been faithful to her mission, because her children, set apart from all other people to serve God's Holy Kingdom, have turned aside, disobeyed His commandments——

JOANNA: There I am in agreement with you.

MILCAH: Was not everything that is now happening foretold by divine messengers—prophet after prophet, uttering God's own words of warning?

JOANNA: Yes, indeed. All that is part of my Faith.

MILCAH: If the fools had only heeded these warnings!

JOANNA (softly assenting): Instead, they persecuted the prophets.

MILCAH: Yes—as they persecuted the last of them, the prophet of this ill-fated generation: Rabbi Johanan ben Zakkai!

JOANNA (murmuring the formula): May his soul rest in peace. . . .

MILCAH: May his message live after him! There we part company, I think. My brother taught that the first duty of every Jew was to order his conduct scrupulously according to the Law of Moses—our great Torah which satisfies all the needs of this life, but which has become old-fashioned and a hindrance to those who prefer to take a short cut to salvation! How many times have I not heard him at the Great Synagogue—until his mouth was stopped!—pleading with the tears rolling down his cheeks: "You would not submit to the ordinances of a loving God, and so now you have to submit to the decrees of a foreign tyrant. You grudged your half-shekels for the upkeep of the Temple, and so now you have to pay fifteen shekels into the Treasury of your enemies. You would not repair the roads to enable your pilgrims to observe the Holy Festivals, and so now you have to repair the fortifications and watch-towers of your oppressors!"

JOANNA (tactfully): He was a fine preacher. He was a good man.

MILCAH: Only not good enough to belong to your community!

JOANNA: He was honoured by all of us for his noble stand against the Sadducees when they murdered our Bishop James. And as we loved and prayed for him in life, so now shall we mourn for him and revere his memory. . . . And so we come into agreement again.

[DAVID has entered through the curtains. A man in the early thirties, studious-looking, with a closely trimmed beard. Like MILCAH, he shows signs of strain.

DAVID (gently, conscious of a visitor's presence): Auntie?

MILCAH (rising instantly): Am I wanted?

DAVID: Please. (*As* JOANNA, *too, rises.*) Your pardon for interrupting.

[MILCAH *is already on her way out. He is about to follow her.*

JOANNA: David !

DAVID (*turning, startled*): *You !*

JOANNA: Don't go, please. I won't keep you long.

DAVID (*exhibiting deep emotion*): After all these years !

JOANNA: Are you angry with me ?

DAVID: Angry ? Would you allow me——? (*He approaches her.*)

JOANNA: Of course. (*They embrace tenderly.*) I was so afraid you wouldn't want to speak to me.

DAVID: Yes, for a long time I felt bitterness, but all that has completely burnt itself out. Now everything is clear and natural between us as formerly—everything (*in wonderment*) since yesterday.

JOANNA: Since yesterday ? That's strange ! So often since our ways parted I have determined to call here, but always some inner conflict held me back. Until yesterday. . . .

DAVID: You mean the news about my father ?

JOANNA: No, it was before I heard that. During a meeting at our synagogue. A sudden decision.

DAVID (*looking at her*): You haven't changed.

JOANNA: That seemed to surprise your aunt. Surely *you* could not have expected me ever to recant——?

DAVID: I meant your looks haven't changed. So many people one meets nowadays have changed almost beyond recognition.

JOANNA: It is fear that has changed them.

DAVID: Yes. Fear. Have you not been in fear, Joanna ?

JOANNA: Sometimes. Never for very long—except once. That was a long time ago when our James was martyred. It shook us all. But it passed.

DAVID: And now—with all these accumulating horrors ?

JOANNA: I don't count momentary panic—the fears that catch you when you are off guard. One has only to keep one's armour close at hand.

DAVID: Tell me this, Joanna. Do our psalms mean to you what they did in the old days when we used to sing them in unison ?

JOANNA: Oh, David, of course. As though anything—anything real—had been taken away !

DAVID: How near to you I feel, even now.

166

JOANNA: Perhaps we have never really been separated. In God we remained united.

DAVID: Yes. . . . God forgive me if I speak a heresy, but is not that enough? Does all the rest—do all our differences—matter so much? (JOANNA *is silent*.) To you they still matter. You would have me become a Nazarene even now!

JOANNA: Surely it is natural to want to share one's deepest experiences with a soul mate?

DAVID: One day we will share everything . . . on the day of resurrection.

JOANNA: And meanwhile? Yesterday—and to-day—and to-morrow.

DAVID: Yesterday your decision. To-day reunion. To-morrow is with God. It is unwise to plan even for the morrow in a time like this. Perhaps we shall not meet again to-morrow.

JOANNA (*slowly*): Perhaps not ever again, in the flesh.

DAVID: That thought prompted your decision to visit me?

JOANNA: That thought and another thought—that possibility and another possibility . . . which I would now broach to you.

DAVID (*shaking his head*): There is not much time.

JOANNA: There is God's time for all things. Our time presses here in Jerusalem—that I know. It is my theme. Before many months or weeks, the City will be encircled by Roman armies. The siege will take a heavy toll, and few who live to the end of it will survive the holocaust that must follow. Have you considered that prospect in all its bearings?

DAVID (*unsteadily*): Did you come here to torture me?

JOANNA: David, I have come here to save you—to save you from that fate.

DAVID (*recoiling*): What are you saying?

JOANNA: I am inviting you to escape with me from Jerusalem.

DAVID (*stammering*): Joanna, but you must know that—isn't possible.

JOANNA: I know that all the gates of the city are closely guarded and that the guards have orders to send a spear through the back of anyone attempting to pass out of them. I wasn't proposing that we should escape that way.

DAVID: There is no other way out of the City.

JOANNA: A way has been found. If you will trust yourself to my guidance——

DAVID (*staring at her*): Am I dreaming all this? That you should come to me with a plan of escape—to-day of all days!

JOANNA: The chance will not come again. Say you will take it, David.

[*He continues to stare at her, but is brought down to actuality by a knocking at the front door—two followed by three short raps.*

DAVID (*quietly*): And there is my answer!

JOANNA: It is someone you have been waiting for?

DAVID: Eliezer and Joshua—two of my father's disciples. (*Moving to the door.*) They have been attending to his funeral arrangements.

JOANNA (*as he unbolts the door*): I can wait. I will wait here all day if necessary.

DAVID (*cryptically*): It will not be necessary. (*He throws open the door.*) At last! (*He admits* ELIEZER *and* JOSHUA, *a queerly complementary couple.* ELIEZER *is a human thinking machine, middle-aged, physically frail, severe of aspect, and habitually silent, as though unwilling to dissipate his brain-energy in mere language.* JOSHUA *is younger, muscular, genial-looking and an easy talker. Both are pale and somewhat excited.*) Both unharmed, thank God! (*He closes the door after them.*)

JOSHUA (*expressively*): In the shelter of the wing!

DAVID: You were not molested on the way?

JOSHUA: Twice we ran into bands of irregulars. We seemed to be invisible to them. In the shelter of the wing, all the time.

DAVID: And your mission? Well?

JOSHUA: Well, indeed! (ELIEZER *is glancing uneasily at* JOANNA.) It is your kinswoman? (DAVID *smiles reassurance.*) Very well. Our petition forthwith granted—the token made out, countersigned by the General, and actually handed over—all within an hour!

DAVID: Your fiery tongue has worked a wonder!

JOSHUA: My fiery tongue? Say rather the weight of the cemented cistern! (ELIEZER, *thus alluded to, is growing restive.*) In short, the arrangements can go forward whenever we will—God permitting.

DAVID (*thoughtfully*): Yes. . . . Will you report within? You will find my aunt there. . . . I will join you shortly. (*He has shown them out, and now returns to deal with* JOANNA.)

JOANNA: So the funeral will take place, all being well, before nightfall?

DAVID: The preparations have been completed.

JOANNA: And after that, David? (*He looks up.*) After the funeral? (*He does not answer.*) After that, you will be free!

DAVID (*smiling*): You think so?

JOANNA: I mean, free to come with me—free to be saved ! While your father lived, I know you would never have deserted him. But now—once you have seen his body to its resting place, surely you would not choose to remain here like a trapped animal? What purpose could it serve? Would your father himself have wished it?

DAVID (*slowly*): My father would not wish me to go with you.

JOANNA: I see. (*Losing her control.*) So he is to come between us once again, even from the grave.

DAVID (*protesting*): Joanna !

JOANNA: Yes, why should we pretend ? But for your father's influence you would have followed me that other time—followed me to those meetings, and learnt about the Messiah—and perhaps in time followed *Him*.

DAVID: Never, never !

JOANNA: I know you better. You are not a whole-hearted Pharisee. You haven't that temperament. You are just your father's son—and weak, weak ! (*Suddenly recovering.*) Forgive me, David. All that isn't what I meant to say. (*With an effort.*) Forget what separates us—consider only what we have in common: remember that we are allies—nay, fellow prisoners, with a deep and pure love uniting us——

DAVID (*warmly*): Joanna ! God knows I wish you every blessing that life can provide ! I pray that your plan may lead you to safety, and to the enjoyment of many many years of peace ! (*Overcome with emotion.*) I can say no more.

JOANNA (*desperately*): I will not take that for an answer! (*There is a loud knock at the door.*) Nor that! Not for all your father's following!

DAVID (*on the alert*): This is a different kind of visitor, I fear.

JOANNA (*subdued*): You have enemies, I know.

[*Renewed knocking, and a loud voice from without.*

THE VOICE: Hullo, there ! David ! David, son of Johanan !

DAVID (*calling back*): Who is it ?

THE VOICE: Ben Batiah.

JOANNA: Your cousin—that madman !

DAVID (*grimly*): Yes—now one of our popular leaders ! (*Further knocking.*) He must not be kept waiting.

JOANNA: He has come perhaps as a member of the family.

DAVID (*half to himself*): We shall soon see. . . . (*He opens the door to a gigantic and coarse-featured warrior in all the panoply of his trade.*) Come in, Ben Batiah.

BEN BATIAH: Just what I was going to do ! (*He strides into the room, and stares at* JOANNA.) I know your face !

JOANNA: I was once betrothed to David.

BEN BATIAH: Of course. I remember. Joanna! (*With a guffaw.*) The damsel who used to try and save all our souls! You've got over that nonsense by now, I dare say! (*Turning to* DAVID.) I heard about poor Uncle. Long life and all that.

DAVID: Thank you.

BEN BATIAH: Auntie bearing up all right?

DAVID: She's not very well.

BEN BATIAH: Naturally. (*Awkwardly.*) A sad business, of course. The end was a bit sudden, eh?

DAVID: His heart had been weak for some time.

BEN BATIAH: Is that so? (*A pause.*)

DAVID (*Edging towards the front door*): It was kind of you to come.

BEN BATIAH: It was the wife's idea, if you want to know. She seemed to think it was the correct thing.

DAVID: I expect you have your hands full now.

BEN BATIAH (*brightening up*): You're right there, old man! More vermin to be exterminated, eh? We're ready for them! If old Simon thinks he's going to shift us from the Temple Mount, he's made the mistake of his life! You can take it from me, we shall have the situation under control by to-morrow.

DAVID: The attack hasn't opened yet?

BEN BATIAH: You wouldn't find me here if it had! We know pretty well what's going on inside their Councils, though. There's not much that escapes the ears of our Secret Service!

DAVID: That is well known.

BEN BATIAH (*with a grin*): The old man knew, eh? (DAVID *controls his temper.*) When are you burying him, by the way?

DAVID: As soon as we can. (*Hastily.*) We are not making any announcement.

BEN BATIAH: Sarah asked me to find out.

DAVID: He expressed a wish that only his disciples and pupils should be present.

BEN BATIAH: There won't be much of a crowd, then!

DAVID: No, there aren't many of us.

BEN BATIAH: Oh! So you include yourself among them, do you? I ought to have known that, I suppose.

DAVID: Why should you? Our paths diverged so many years ago.

BEN BATIAH: Yes. And so now they're turning you into a learned man of Israel—teaching you to goggle over ancient manuscripts and recite your blessings for every occasion, and lay down the law as a cure for insomnia ! And to think I was brought up to believe there was something praiseworthy in all that kind of thing ! " *You'll* never make a Rabbi," they used to tell me at school. And, by the Temple, they were right !

DAVID (*politely*) : Please give my remembrances to your wife.

BEN BATIAH (*taking the cue*) : That's right. . . . And you give Sarah's to Auntie Milcah. . . . Was there anything else ? (*Recollecting.*) Oh, where are you burying Uncle ?

DAVID (*a shade diffidently*) : He is to be buried in the Old Ground.

BEN BATIAH (*in surprise*) : What ? The Old—— ? But that's beyond the outer wall ?

DAVID : We have obtained permission.

BEN BATIAH : From whom ?

DAVID : From the High Priest, ratified by the General—by John of Giskala, in his own hand. . . . (*In explanation.*) It was my father's particular wish to be buried beside his master Hillel.

BEN BATIAH : Ah, Hillel—the great Hillel. I might have known his name would be dragged into it ! How it used to rile me as a child—the way that fellow's name would be dished up as a kind of testimonial to my uncle's importance. " Don't you dare to make fun of your Uncle Johanan ! Remember he occupies the chair of the great Hillel ! " And then there was that other one— the great Shammai. Didn't Uncle sit in his chair as well ?

DAVID : That is so. He occupied the chairs of both the great schools.

BEN BATIAH : At the same time, eh ? (*With his guffaw.*) How he managed it beats me !

DAVID : The names mean nothing to you now ?

BEN BATIAH : What, Hillel and Shammai—and all the other old dodderers, past, present and future ? Oh, yes. Their names mean something. I'll tell you just what they mean to me. They mean subversive opinions, defeatism, playing into Rome's hands ! (*Snapping his fingers.*) That for the lot of them ! . . . Give me a man with neat fingers to slit a Roman throat.

[MILCAH *has returned to the room. She is in tears.*

DAVID : Here is our aunt.

BEN BATIAH : Oh, beg pardon ! (*Turning to her.*) Well, Auntie. Long life to you, as they say.

MILCAH (*as he pecks her cheek*) : Peace, my nephew.

BEN BATIAH: Peace? No, thank you—not peace Auntie! Not peace while there's a Roman left on Jewish soil.

DAVID: I beg you, cousin—no politics to-day.

BEN BATIAH (*exploding*): Politics! Politics! That's all it means to you people!

DAVID (*exerting himself*): Forgive me, cousin. (*To* MILCAH.) Ben Batiah, in spite of his important military duties, has called to pay his respects——

BEN BATIAH: His wife's respects, if you please. Don't think I want to take the credit. Personally, I don't see any sense in these pious duty calls. Either you want to visit people or you don't. As I said to Sarah, " I don't believe I've ever been in that house five minutes without treading on somebody's corns." It was on the last occasion, if I remember rightly, that I was treated for my sins to a full-length sermon from the late lamented——

MILCAH (*with compressed lips*): As a result of which you reported your uncle as a spy!

BEN BATIAH: Not a spy, Auntie—merely one of those pacifist cranks that it's safest to keep muzzled in a time of national emergency. I have reason to believe that my recommendation on the subject was followed by appropriate action.

MILCAH (*boiling over*): *You* recommended that Rabbi Johanan ben Zakkai should be muzzled!

DAVID (*apprehensively*): Auntie! Auntie!

BEN BATIAH: There you are! I've put my foot in it again as usual!

MILCAH: *You* took it upon yourself to suppress God's spokesman in a time of national emergency!

DAVID: Now, now, Auntie——

MILCAH (*in withering scorn*): You should have done your work more thoroughly—you should have obliterated the word of God altogether! Yes, muzzle every righteous man left in Israel, burn every scroll of the law you can lay hands on—you will never efface God's curse upon you that way: God's curse pronounced upon your father, Cain!

BEN BATIAH (*roused*): That's going too far! Perhaps you don't realize who you are talking to?

MILCAH: I am talking to my great bloodthirsty lout and ignorant booby of a nephew! And I tell him to get out of this house double quickly!

BEN BATIAH (*livid*): We'll see about that! Give orders to me, would you? You'll take back your insults this instant, or——

(*The sound of the horns, signalling another alarm, arrests him. For a moment or two he wavers, but the call from without prevails, and he pulls himself together.*) One thing at a time ! (*Turning to* MILCAH.) Very well—you order me from the house, and I obey. You will see me back again—sooner than you expect, perhaps—on a duty visit of a different order. (DAVID *has already opened the door for him, and bolts it after him. There is an uneasy silence. The horn signal dies away.*)

MILCAH (*still fuming*) : I'm not afraid of his threats !

DAVID : He knows about the burial. (*She quails.*) At least we have had warning.

MILCAH (*in subdued anxiety*) : Yes, you'll have to start at once.

JOANNA (*coming forward*) : Surely not while there's an alarm on ?

MILCAH (*disconcerted*) : What, are *you* still here ?

JOANNA (*vaguely*) : If I could be of some help . . .

MILCAH (*curtly*) : You can't. You are in the way. (*To* DAVID.) As soon as the " All Clear " sounds, then. I'll see that they're ready. (*Turning at the curtains.*) I'm sorry I lost my temper with him.

DAVID : We're all of us in God's hands, Auntie.

[*She disappears. He stands still, torn by conflicting emotions.*

JOANNA (*echoing*) : In God's hands—all of us. . . . Yes. (*Facing him.*) Noah was in God's hands when he entered the Ark. Had he remained outside, God would not have spared him. If you remain in Jerusalem, you will be putting yourself in Ben Batiah's hands.

DAVID (*desperately*) : I can't discuss it with you, Joanna.

JOANNA : Why not ? You have discussed the subject with others often enough!

DAVID (*confused*) : I don't understand you.

JOANNA : Then I will speak plainly. Your father, before he died, made more than one attempt to escape from Jerusalem.

DAVID : You have heard that ? From whom ?

JOANNA : Call it prisoners' gossip, if you like—perhaps no more than guesswork. Everyone knows your father lived only for his school—the famous " Great House "——

DAVID : Yes, the Great House of the Torah, a sacred trust—a torch to be kept alight and handed on——

JOANNA : As could never have been accomplished in what will be left of Jerusalem after the flood has subsided. Surely it is natural that your father should have sought, before it was too late, to remove his school to a place of safety. (DAVID *is silent.*) Had he succeeded, you would have gone with him—into his Ark. But he failed, and he is now dead——

173

DAVID: And so you would have me go with you into another Ark—serve a strange Noah—the leader of your sect, perhaps?

JOANNA (*with a smile*): How I used to snap at you for calling it a sect!

DAVID: It no longer matters so much?

JOANNA: No. The movement has grown to such dimensions——

DAVID: Grown? I had almost forgotten it existed. One had heard nothing of you for so long.

JOANNA: Since the crisis came upon us, we have been working like moles—underground. But we have come to see that in Jerusalem our ministry can be of no further avail. We had our great hour and that passed, and we were left behind. We are now no more than an outpost on the fringe of a world empire. Do you know where the heart of that Empire has been established, David?

DAVID: In Syria, perhaps?

JOANNA: In Rome.

DAVID: Rome? What, under Cæsar's very nose? Or under his protection, perhaps? You have made your peace with Cæsar?

JOANNA: We have invaded Rome. We are in Cæsar's citadel. We are going to conquer Rome.

DAVID: Listen! (*A gathering tumult has become audible.*) It's fighting this time!

JOANNA (*more loudly*): We are going to conquer Cæsar, but not with Cæsar's weapons. Let them fight if they must!

DAVID: Yes. . . . (*Returning to her.*) And so it is for Rome that your Ark is bound?

JOANNA: Not so. There is no place for us in Rome. We belong to the land of Israel. We are the church of the Judæans—the earliest of all the Christian churches. And we have our marching orders. (*Raising her voice above a crescendo of confused clamour.*) " And ye shall hear of wars and rumours of wars and many shall stumble and shall betray one another, and shall hate one another. And the love of many shall wax cold, but he that shall endure unto the end shall be saved. And the good news of the Kingdom shall be preached in the whole world for a testimony unto all the nations, and after that shall the end come. Then let them which be in Judæa flee unto the mountains——"

[*The tumult is dying down.*

DAVID: It is growing quieter again!

JOANNA: Yes. Soon they will be blowing the " All Clear." . . .

DAVID: And so you are making for the mountains?

JOANNA: We have planned with care. . . . I am trusting you with our secret, David, as I believe you would trust me. The moles have found a tunnel-way out of the City. Pella is our destination. One of our party has elected to stay behind to nurse a sick brother. I obtained leave of Symeon—our Bishop—to offer you his place . . . Oh, say you will come !

DAVID: There will be work for you to do at Pella ?

JOANNA: Yes, there will be work. We have our synagogue there.

DAVID: And what work have you to offer a pupil of Rabbi Johanan ben Zakkai ?

JOANNA (*desperately*): What good can you do by remaining here ?

DAVID (*deliberately*): I shall do no good by remaining here, Joanna.

JOANNA: You are keeping something back from me !

[*Before he can reply, the curtains behind him are drawn aside and there is a shuffling of feet beyond.*

DAVID (*tensely*): Now my lips are finally sealed.

[*Preceded by* ELIEZER, JOSHUA, *and three other sturdy men, all sombrely clad, slowly advance into the room, supporting on their shoulders a crudely-carpentered plain black coffin.*

JOANNA (*in despair*): The coffin !

DAVID: The Shofar has sounded, without our hearing—— ?

JOSHUA (*answering him*): A voice has commanded. (*To his comrades.*) On the table. Gently. Gently.

[*They lower the coffin on to a dwarf table in the centre of the room.*

DAVID (*meanwhile, instructing* JOANNA): You are in the presence of the five disciples of the Rabban. Their names shall live ! Rabbi Eliezer ben Hyrcanus, Rabbi Joshua ben Hananiah, Rabbi José ben Halafta, Rabbi Simeon ben Nathaniel, Rabbi Elezazar ben Arach!

JOSHUA (*to his comrades*): Keep your stations ! All is now in readiness.

JOANNA (*boldly*): I am not afraid of them. Until the Shofar has sounded, time remains, and, with time, there is hope. I speak openly before all. (*Addressing the disciples.*) Why should I not ? My home is in Jerusalem like yours. We speak the same tongue, were nurtured in the same Holy Scriptures, seek the one truth which is the same for all. We know by the light of that truth that our city is doomed, and justly doomed. And with the city goes the Temple, and all that the Temple has stood for. It is the passing of the old Israel. Hear me ! A new Israel has already come to birth—an Israel not confined to a building, or a walled city, or a land with marked frontiers, but inheritor of God's promise to our Father

Abraham that in his seed would all the nations of the world be blessed. That seed—a seed of the spirit—scattered far and wide, is now bursting with new life at Antioch, at Corinth, at Alexandria, at Rome—wherever the old life has been lived since Adam fell. David, (*turning to him*) will you not, by uniting with this spirit, save your own life ? Or will you rather cling to a mere corpse ?

DAVID (*distinctly*): I will rather cling to the body of Rabbi Johanan ben Zakkai, in whose keeping is the Torah received by Moses from God Himself !

JOANNA (*answering him*): God has sent deliverance from that Torah through a greater than Moses. (*A gasp of horror. She raises her voice.*) Your Torah, I say, fittingly with (*pointing to the coffin*) the last of its guardians, is dead !

[*There is a pause, broken only by deep breathing that reflects the shock of those announcements. Then suddenly the long, sustained note of the " All Clear " signal complicates the tension. The sound dies away. No one moves. After a slight interval,* MILCAH *bursts in.*

MILCAH (*staring about her*): No one stirring ? Have I dreamt that the " All Clear " was signalled ? What is keeping you all—when haste may be all-important—— ?

[*Bewildered eyes turn to* ELIEZER *for guidance. After a momentary indecision, he raises his arm, and, without more ado,* JOSHUA *and his fellow-bearers stoop down to raise the coffin on to their shoulders again.*

DAVID (*in a whisper*): Farewell, Joanna.

[*The coffin is hoisted aloft.*

JOANNA (*defeated, staring before her*): Dead, dead, dead. . . .

[*The burial party, starting to move forward, is arrested by a muffled voice from the coffin.*

RABBI JOHANAN BEN ZAKKAI (*unseen*): Stop ! (*The lid of the coffin is raised, and a venerable head entwined with massive phylacteries, emerges.*) Is no one to confute the heretic ?

MILCAH: Johanan ! Brother !

[JOANNA, *stifling a cry, has recoiled.* DAVID *hastens to her side.*

RABBI JOHANAN BEN ZAKKAI (*sitting bolt upright, and quoting Hillel*): " If I speak not for myself, who will speak for me ? And if for myself alone, what am I ? And if not now, when ? " (*Fixing* JOANNA.) Hear me, daughter of the New Israel !

DAVID (*interrupting*): Father, release me from my oath that I may first explain to her——

MILCAH: Silence for the Rabban !

RABBI JOHANAN BEN ZAKKAI: This Torah which you say is dead, as I am, was taught to me by two great Masters. I learned from them no more than what a dog can lap from the ocean. Yet if the entire Heavens were parchment, every human being a scribe, and all the trees of the forests pens, it would not suffice to transcribe what I learnt from my Masters.

DAVID: Father, please let me explain——

JOANNA: There is no need, David. I see now that there is more than one way of escaping from the city, and that my errand was a vain one. (*She turns to go.* MILCAH *makes a movement.*) Never fear! Your secret will be as safe with me, as mine with David. Farewell!

RABBI JOHANAN BEN ZAKKAI: Stay ! (*He addresses her.*) You have said truly: there is more than one way of escaping. For you, the way of the Nazarene. I do not judge you— your Bishop Jacob the Just was my friend in youth, and his death was a pain to me. All ways to the Kingdom are hard—that Kingdom which is shared by the righteous of all nations. . . . I know only one Israel, an old nation, as I am old, but that there is life left in that nation, my life is the proof. Hillel, as he lay dying, blessed me with the words, " Father of Coming Generations." In that blessing, strong is my old age, I go forth with my scholars, a faithful remnant, to transplant the tree of the Torah into a new soil.

[*There is a loud knocking at the outer door.*

JOSHUA (*springing to the alert*): Let no one answer !

BEN BATIAH (*without*): Open this door !

DAVID (*between his teeth*): Ben Batiah ! He has lost no time !

BEN BATIAH (*between knocks*): Open, I say ! There must be someone there !

MILCAH (*wringing her hands*): What did I tell you ? We have left it too late ! (*Further knocking.*) Now all will come out !

RABBI JOHANAN BEN ZAKKAI (*in a piercing hiss*): Woman, where is your faith ? (*Sharply, to the men.*) The procession will form at once. (ELIEZER *stations himself at the head, facing the front door.* DAVID *falls in at the rear.*) Remember my directions. Only let the fear of God be as strong in you as the fear of flesh and blood. (*Turning to* MILCAH, *more gently.*) For the last time, sister, farewell ! (*Finally, to* ELIEZER.) I give you leave to disturb my prayers when you have reached the Roman camp.

[*With these words, he settles himself back in the coffin, carefully closing the lid over him.*

MILCAH (*murmuring in awe*): Light of Israel, pillar of the sanctuary, strong hammer !

Ben Batiah (*knocking furiously*): Open, or I'll put a battering ram to the door !

[Eliezer *almost nonchalantly throws the front door wide open. Simultaneously his comrades begin a subdued murmuring of Psalm XCI, and* Milcah *breaks into a loud wailing appropriate to a funeral ceremony.* Joanna *retires to the back of the scene.* Ben Batiah *enters with a drawn sword.*

Ben Batiah (*glaring round*): So I am in time. . . . (*A loud " ssh " from* Milcah.) Silence, everyone. I am in authority here !

Joshua (*in a low voice*): We are about to start—as you see——

Ben Batiah: As I am delighted to see ! I feared I might arrive too late owing to a slight engagement elsewhere, that has now terminated satisfactorily. (*The funeral party commence to edge forward.*) Don't move there ! (*They hesitate. Peremptorily.*) Stop, I say ! Set down the coffin.

Joshua: By what right, may we ask—— ?

Ben Batiah: By the right of a Captain of the Patriot Guards ! Let there be no mistake ! I shall cut down the first man—or woman—who disobeys my orders. (*Roaring.*) Set down the coffin, I say ! (*With* Eliezer's *signified consent, it is lowered once more on to the table.* Eliezer *discreetly closes the front door during the procedure.*) That's better. Now, a few questions regarding this proposed expedition beyond the city walls. Is my cousin David there ? (David *steps forward.*) I understood from you that the burial would be attended by all of the late Rabbi's disciples and pupils. (David *inclines his head.*) There are here present, not counting yourself, exactly five men. (*Sarcastically.*) Are you not able to muster even a congregational quorum ?

David: Other pupils are waiting to join the procession.

Ben Batiah: How many ? You had better be accurate.

David: Fifteen more.

Ben Batiah: Where are they waiting ?

David: At the Beth-ha-Midrash.

Ben Batiah: I see. That makes twenty-one males in all. . . . And you say you have a pass authorizing this exodus ?

Joshua (*intervening*): It is perfectly in order.

Ben Batiah: Is it in your possession ? (Joshua *does not answer.*) Will you show it to me ? (*A pause.*) I am not to be trifled with ! I demand to see the pass. (*As* Joshua *makes no movement.*) Produce it instantly !

Milcah (*in a hoarse whisper*): If you never want to see it again !

BEN BATIAH (*without turning*) : There is a penalty for inciting to resist a Patriot.

MILCAH (*confronting him*) : Answer me ! Are you wanting to *see* the pass, or to confiscate it ?

BEN BATIAH (*mockingly*) : How well you know your nephew, dear Auntie !

MILCAH : Who doesn't know Ben Batiah ? Aren't you the most famous man in Jerusalem ? Haven't you made your name a stinking byword for the disease called Patriotism ?

BEN BATIAH (*with grim composure*) : Have you anything further to say ?

MILCAH (*thoroughly worked up*) : Isn't it you our undernourished children have to thank for the destruction of the public granaries ?

BEN BATIAH : I thought that would be coming next ! If you want to know, it was my own idea, carried out on my own responsibility. And I'm not ashamed of it. Everyone knows hungry people make the best fighters.

MILCAH (*laughing*) : He's not ashamed of his crimes. He's proud of himself !

BEN BATIAH (*furiously to* JOSHUA) : Give me that pass—or by Heaven you'll pay with your life ! (MILCAH *again laughs scornfully. He hisses at her.*) I'll deal with you presently.

[*On a sudden " inspiration,"* JOANNA *comes forward.*

JOANNA (*urgently*) : Deal with her now, Ben Batiah ! Tell me this: is it legal to hoard food ?

BEN BATIAH (*rising to the bait*) : Legal ? What do you mean ? Food-hoarding is punishable with death !

JOANNA (*turning to* MILCAH) : Then I can pay back the grudge I've owed you all these years ! (*To* BEN BATIAH, *dramatically.*) I denounce that woman. Her cellar is full of foodstuffs.

MILCAH (*in amazement*) : Its a lie ! The cellar's empty !

JOANNA : Perhaps you'd allow the Captain to see for himself ?

MILCAH (*playing up, as she suddenly " twigs "*) : Certainly not. He must take my word for it.

JOANNA : And give you an opportunity of removing everything ?

BEN BATIAH : Ha ! We'll see about that ! Where is the cellar ?

JOANNA (*pointing*) : Just through the door, sir. (MILCAH *is barring the way.*) I'll open it for you ! (*She darts round to do so.*)

BEN BATIAH (*brushing* MILCAH *aside*) : Out of my way ! (*He rushes impetuously through the door which* JOANNA *holds open for him.*)

MILCAH (*as* JOANNA *quietly closes and bolts the door behind him*) :

Good for the Nazarene! Bravo! (*She siezes* JOANNA *by the hands.*) And I told her she was in the way! (*She bursts into exultant laughter.*)

JOANNA: God forgive me such lying. . . . I don't know what came over me.

JOSHUA: The cunning of wisdom came over you. As it is said, " and the fool shall be servant to the wise." (*He catches* ELIEZER'S *eye.*) But now—forward at last! (*He and his fellow-bearers raise the coffin on their shoulders again.*)

JOANNA: Good luck, David! (*From this point the pace of the speeches quickens.*)

DAVID (*embracing her*): God give you as prosperous a send-off on your journey! (*He goes to* MILCAH.) And you, Auntie. (*Pressing her hand.*) Would we could take you with us!

MILCAH: What, transplant my old bones, would you? No, thank you. My heart wouldn't stand it, for one thing. But it goes deeper than that. Jerusalem, in life or death for me, were King Solomon himself to bid me fly with him! (BEN BATIAH *commences to bang on the cellar door, demanding to be let out.*) There's a nice fat rat to keep me company!

JOSHUA (*as* ELIEZER *throws open the door*): Farewell, Jerusalem!

[*The party, which has " fallen in " as before, breaks into the Ninety-first Psalm, this time with raised voices to counteract the noise proceeding from the cellar.* ELIEZER *raises his arm as a signal. With a note of quiet confidence in their voices, the procession moves forward, leaving* MILCAH *and* JOANNA *alone.* JOANNA *turns to* MILCAH *as if offering assistance, but is dismissed with a firm but friendly gesture, followed by a kiss at the door.* JOANNA *departs, and as the hammering and shouting of* BEN BATIAH *becomes louder,* MILCAH *hastily closes and bolts the door behind her. She then settles herself with a sigh of relaxation to savour the threats and curses of the defeated enemy, presently bursting into paroxysms of hysterical laughter.*

CURTAIN

NOTE

Yes, Rabbi Johanan ben Zakkai is a historical figure of some significance. Sayings of his (some quoted in my dialogue) and of his five disciples are recorded in a Talmudic treatise known as " Ethics of the Fathers " which forms part of the common Jewish Prayer Book. The story of his escape from Jerusalem in a coffin may be apocryphal, but it is at least certain that he was successfully evacuated before the fall of the City, and that he re-established his school, by leave of Titus, in Jabneh (or Jamnia) near Jaffa, and so kept Judaism alive. The flight of the Jewish-Christian community from Jerusalem to Pella probably took place somewhat earlier, but the traditions of the Early Church are as vague in dating events as the Rabbinical records, and both exoduses may have happened about the same time. The Rabbi is known to have had a son (who pre-deceased him), and the monstrous Ben Batiah, who burnt the granaries to encourage the populace to fight, is said to have been his nephew.

21